THE WRECKS OF
SCAPA FLOW

THE WRECKS OF
SCAPA FLOW

compiled by
DAVID M. FERGUSON

with underwater photographs by
Bob Michelson

and a historical preface by
Prof. Friedrich Ruge,
former Head of the West German Federal Navy

The Orkney Press
in association with Stromness Museum
1985

The publishers wish to express their thanks to the many people who helped in the publication of this volume. They would warmly welcome any additional information that might be of help in future editions.

Published by The Orkney Press Ltd., 72 Victoria Street, Stromness, Orkney in association with Stromness Museum and with the assistance of the Highlands and Islands Development Board and Orkney Islands Council.

ISBN 0 907618 06 5

Printed by The Kirkwall Press, "The Orcadian" Office, Victoria Street, Kirkwall, Orkney.
Colour by Nevisprint, Fort William

CONTENTS

PHOTOGRAPHS
Black and white

Colour (by Bob Michelson)

FOREWORD

When the German High Seas Fleet was scuttled in Scapa Flow in 1919, few people could have foreseen the long-term effects for Orkney. For the Admiralty, the wrecks created a seemingly permanent hazard in their spacious northern anchorage: "Where they lie, they will rest and rust — there can be no question of salvage."

The shores of Scapa Flow were littered with all sorts of debris from the ships, and it was second nature to Orcadians to gather it up for use or ornament in the time-honoured tradition of beach-combing.

The possibility of salvage presented a challenge to commercial interests. Chief among these was the firm of Cox and Danks, whose breathtaking feats brought pressmen and photographers from afar to capture the moment when, pumped full of air, the capsized hulls reared like huge leviathans above the surface of the Flow. Cox and Danks, and later Metal Industries Ltd., provided employment for many during the lean years of the '20s and '30s.

Salvage operations were halted during World War II, but they continued afterwards, on a smaller scale. In the nuclear age, the submerged armourplate, protected from radiation by the depth of sea-water above it for many years, was the perfect material for nuclear reactor shields. Nundy Marine Metals and Scapa Flow Salvage employed skin-divers to break up the wrecks on the sea-bed.

By the 1970s, the historical interest of the wrecks was becoming apparent. A general exhibition on Scapa Flow at Stromness Museum in 1970 included among other items from the sunken fleet a flag from *SMS Hindenburg*. The lucrative 'mine' of valuable metals was beginning to be seen in another light — as one of the world's great war fleets which could one day rank in interest with the Spanish Armada.

The tourist boom of the '70s brought back to Orkney many who had been stationed here during the wars. In response to their interest, the Museum decided to mount a major exhibition called "The Salving of the German Fleet."

Local inquiries revealed many souvenirs from the fleet which had been acquired by salvage workers. China, silver, hatbands, flags and weapons flowed in to the museum. Superb photographs by the local photographer Willie Hourston were 'blown up' from the original plates. After months of preparation, the exhibition opened in June of 1974.

All summer long, unprecedented crowds thronged the museum. What had been planned as a temporary exhibition became a permanent attraction, the booklet accompanying it a best-seller.

Visitors to the exhibition have included Professor Friedrich Ruge, a distinguished figure in the history of the German Navy, who served in the Grand Fleet during the internment and scuttling and wrote the book *Scapa Flow 1919.* Professor Ruge has kindly contributed a personal reminiscence for this publication. During a lull in the seal cull of 1978, Dan van der Vat, then covering the event for *The Times,* visited the museum and was inspired to write *The Grand Scuttle,* an account of the events leading up to the sinking of the fleet.

Museums are frequently regarded as little more than a convenient place for visitors to pass the time on rainy days. It is seldom realised that good museums can influence the public and boost the economy for the benefit of all. But what can be done is amply demonstrated through Stromness Museum's efforts in awakening public interest in the German wrecks and the subsequent growth of the sub-aqua industry.

In the 1980s, Stromness Museum welcomes a stream of divers who wish to increase their knowledge of the German Fleet. Photographers and film crews from both sides of the Atlantic are a familiar sight in the museum each summer, ensuring ever wider publicity for Orkney's 'sunken treasure'.

Stromness Museum is proud to be associated with The Orkney Press in the publication of this long-awaited guide to the wrecks of Scapa Flow.

BRYCE S. WILSON
11th February 1985   Museums Officer, Orkney

HISTORICAL PREFACE

AN EYE-WITNESS RECALLS THE EVENTS
WHICH LED UP TO THE SCUTTLING
OF THE GERMAN FLEET

(Professor Friedrich Ruge joined the German Navy in April 1914 and served as an officer on the German Fleet during its internment in Scapa Flow. In the course of a long and distinguished career, he served in old ships and modern destroyers, between the wars mostly in mine development and minesweeping. As Senior Officer Minesweepers, in 1940-41, he built up the German naval defence forces from the North Sea to the Spanish frontier. In 1943 he was promoted Vice-Admiral.

From 1956 to 1961 he was Senior Officer of the new German Navy. After retirement, he lectured at Tübingen University and was made an honorary professor. He is still writing and lecturing and does much work for improving understanding within NATO. Professor Ruge visited the German Fleet exhibition at Stromness Museum in July 1982.)

During World War I, to the German Navy Scapa Flow was a distant place affording to the Grand Fleet a first-class position for blockading the northern exit of the North Sea. It was not mentioned when the Armistice of 9th November 1918 stipulated that 10 battleships, 6 battle-cruisers, 8 light cruisers and fifty destroyers were to be interned in a neutral port or, if not available, in one of the Allied countries. This pointed to Scandinavia, but in those troubled times with mutiny and revolution nobody made any enquiries. After hectic work to disarm our ships we just made it to the rendezvous off the Firth of Forth on the morning of 21st November. Our ships were controlled at anchor in the Firth, and then we were simply told to be ready for sea again the next morning.

I was officer of the watch in *B110,* a destroyer ("great torpedo-boat" officially, for in the German Navy all torpedo-craft up to destroyer were named "torpedo-boat") in 4th Half-Flotilla, which together with 3 Half-Flotilla and a "Senior Officer's Boat" formed "II Torpedo-boat Flotilla" of 11 boats. Three had been left in Germany because under repairs. The other eight went to sea again the next day, escorted by British destroyers. Destination was still unknown but became clear from the courses to be steered.

We entered Scapa Flow from the south on a grey November morning and moored in pairs to big buoys in the entrance of Gutter Sound, well protected against westerly gales. The other destroyers moored inside Gutter Sound, the big ships anchored around Cava Island. From our buoy we could see most of them, and also deep into Gutter Sound. A disadvantage was that a British destroyer was always moored to the nearest buoy so that we were under observation all the time. A British Battle Squadron anchored to the east.

Rear-Admiral Ludwig von Reuter was in command of the interned ships, with the battleship *Friedrich der Grosse* as flagship. Life was made difficult for him by the Soldiers' Council, and he moved to the cruiser *Emden.* We were not allowed to fly our flag, but command pennants were permitted. Orders came to reduce the crews to 200 men for battle-cruisers, 175 for battleships, 50 for light cruisers and 20 for torpedo-boats. With these nucleus crews the ships could move at slow speed.

Soon German steamers arrived to take the superfluous men away. The others moved together on the *B110/B112* group for we received oil to heat one boiler for half a day only in four boats. Working hours for keeping our ships in order were from 9 a.m. to 2 p.m. In this time boat traffic between the two groups was allowed, but not with other ships. The islands were taboo.

Soon souvenir-hunters in the guard drifters discovered that the group *B109/B111* was empty every evening and night. We installed a guard, and I had to spend every fourth night there with three of my men. Another problem was food. It had to come from Germany, which was still under blockade, and it was just sufficient in calories, but monotonous and generally tasting of turnips which formed the basis of almost everything. It was a boon that there were swarms of small fish like sprats all around us. These were easily lured with lamps hanging over the water, and caught with makeshift nets. I think, they provided the necessary vitamins. In any case, health was good all the time with the exception of the bad state of the teeth of some of our men. The worst cases had to be sent home. We were to get a German dentist but he could be sent out so late only that he arrived just in time to see the ships sink.

Week after week, month after month, passed without any change in our situation. There was one strong gale from the east which cost us most of our hawsers and fenders. Fortunately, there was no repetition. One day in spring the British collected our wireless receivers. I still have the receipt, and I have met the officer who signed it, later on repeatedly, the last time as a retired Rear-Admiral in the house of the German Ambassador in London.

British papers were now our only source of information. They were a gift of the Admiralty and arrived four days late.

The main task of the officers was to keep the spirit of our men up. In the afternoons and evenings there was ample time for lessons and discussions. Our senior officer spoke excellent English; his mother had come from Scotland. He also gave good Spanish lessons. We others tried our luck in geography and history, mathematics and literature as far as our memory was reliable or books were available. Participation was voluntary and changed frequently, but on the whole we succeeded in making life tolerable. In spring, we started all kinds of games on deck. Playing hide and seek around funnels and masts can be great fun.

In all these activities as well as on watch, I learned much about our men which was useful in later life. It was interesting that the youngest men were much more depressed by being cut off from the outer world than the older ones. Our petty officers were excellent.

We had no connections with the shore and hardly any with the Royal Navy. Relations with the crews of the guard drifters (which carried orders and mail, etc. around) developed well. Before leaving Scapa for another base the captain of one of these drifters invited me to a pleasant and nourishing afternoon tea although this was strictly forbidden.

The situation changed when early in May 1919 the peace conditions were published. No hope to get a single ship back, no hope of coming to a tolerable peace. The attempt to take our ships might be made at any time. Therefore, we prepared them for scuttling. They had grown thick beards of seaweed; opening the sea-valves would not be sufficient. We prepared the valves nevertheless, but disconnected them from the upper deck. In addition we prepared the smashing of seawater pipes and in each boat one condenser for opening. During critical periods there was always a guard on deck. Admiral von Reuter asked for a reduction of the crews, and about half of them could be sent home in the middle of June.

The German Government strictly refused to sign; the Allies announced a state of war to begin at noon on 21st June. Admiral von Reuter sent round an order covering all possibilities from surrender to scuttling. He was not informed that Germany was given two more days to form a government willing to sign. On the morning of 21st June the British warships left Scapa for the first time in seven months, actually for exercises, but we thought for re-entering with reinforcements strong enough to take all our ships simultaneously.

Shortly before 11 a.m. Admiral von Reuter made the signal for scuttling. We opened condensers, valves and pipes, collected our emergency luggage and went into our four cutters. There was no room for the last two men; I put them on a life-raft and towed them behind the others to Fara Island. Shotgun fire of a drifter did no harm, fortunately.

From Fara we watched our ships falling deeper and finally going down or capsizing. *B112* sank shortly after 1 p.m. as the first of the 50 torpedo-boats. Two hours later, most ships had sunk, some were beached. We were towed to the British flagship where we spent the night in a casemate. The next morning the *Royal Oak* took us to Invergordon, and we were sent by train to a prison camp near Oswestry, south of Liverpool. By the end of January 1920, we were back in Germany. But that is another tale.

F. Ruge

25th March, 1984.

Aboard a German destroyer in Scapa Fl

SMS Karlsr

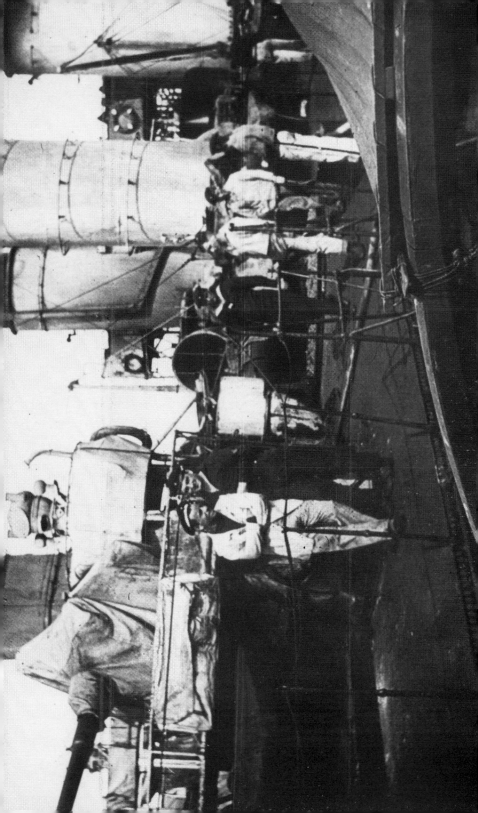

The Wrecks

INTRODUCTION

The idea for compiling this guide came about from a chance conversation in a Stromness bookshop. The owner remarked with regret that he had no book on the wrecks of Scapa Flow for the ever-increasing number of diving visitors who wanted to find out more about the ships. Being at a loose end at the time, I rather naively thought that it would give me something to do. I assumed that the task could not be too difficult as the bulk of the information would have been systematically recorded in various official sources. As the months passed and the material began to accumulate, I realised that some of the information was in fact particularly difficult to obtain, while in other aspects sources, even at times official ones, could be inaccurate or even conflicting. I owe a great debt of gratitude to many people who helped me to clarify many points by putting me in touch with valuable primary source-material. For example, Charles Ledsum of Gibbs Hartley Cooper, London, kindly arranged for me to have access to Lloyds Register of Shipping at Vine Street in London, and without the assistance of Mrs Jean Hood at the Register the detailed section on the blockships could not have been written.

The library staff in Kirkwall and in Stromness unfailingly obtained the obscurest of reference books, and arranged for me to have access to back copies of *The Orcadian* and *The Orkney Herald*. In particular, I would like to thank John Broom of Stromness Library for all his efforts on my behalf.

1S Cöln

ms in Stromness Museum display

I am also most grateful to Nora Kennedy and to Alan Skene for translation of German source-material, and to David Matheson for technical advice. My thanks go too to my brother James, who unearthed a mass of detailed information on individual wrecks, as well as reading various drafts of my manuscript and correcting the more deplorable errors and omissions. Mrs Susan Campbell and Miss Phyllis Sinclair deserve great credit for the skill with which they carried out the unenviable task of typing the various stages of the manuscript.

Bob Michelson of Hamburg, who took all the underwater photographs, provided in a year-long correspondence a vast amount of background information on the German wrecks, and I greatly appreciate all his kind assistance. He also provided detailed up-to-date information on the present condition of the principal wrecks.

I also owe a great debt of gratitude to my editor, Howie Firth, for the many long hours he spent in checking my manuscript and preparing it for publication, and for his guidance and encouragement in the final stages of the project.

The kind assistance of many other individuals and organisations is also greatly appreciated, including:

Capt. E. Bewley, Loganair, Orkney
J. Cook, Kirkwall
R. M. Coppock, Naval Historical Branch, MoD
Anthony Duncan, Burray
Capt. R. Forth, Northern Lighthouse Board
Peter Kenrick and members, St Helen's and
      Widnes Underwater Group
Tam MacPhail, Stromness
Willie Marwick, Stromness
Gunnie Moberg, Stromness
Capt. D. Robertson, Director of Harbours,
      Orkney Island Council
Peter Shearer, Orkney Flying Club
Sandy Tait, Dundas Street, Stromness
Don Temple, Stromness

Mrs R. Traill Thomson, Stromness
Sandy Young, Stromness
Bryce Wilson, Orkney Museums Service
Aberdeen Central Library
Hydrographic Department, MoD, Taunton
Imperial War Museum, London
London Library
National Maritime Museum, Greenwich, London
Naval Historical Branch, MoD, London
Orkney Library Archive, Kirkwall
Public Record Office, Kew, Surrey
Stromness Museum

I should of course stress that the responsibility for any errors is my own, and I would be very glad indeed to hear from anyone who finds a point that needs correcting. According to the Hydrographic Department of the Ministry of Defence, there are no less tham eighty-six charted wrecks in the area covered by Admiralty Chart No. 35 (essentially Scapa Flow), which means that a number of wreck locations still remain to be discovered and located. There is, in fact, much more to be found out about the wrecks of Scapa Flow, and I would very much welcome any additional information that any reader may be able to provide. If this book helps to stimulate more people to find out about these ships and their history, then it will certainly have been well worth the effort of compiling it.

All dimensions are British unless otherwise stated. Tonnage is Gross for merchant ships, and Displacement for warships. Lengths of ships are overall, breadths maximum, and draughts maximum at maximum load. Engine horsepower stated may be IHP (indicated horsepower) for expansion and reciprocating engines, or SHP (shaft horsepower) for turbines and internal combustion engines. Values obtained for engine horse-power during trials are quoted for various warships and indicated accordingly. They are, however, mainly of theoretical interest as they were often obtained under exceptionally favourable conditions which were never likely to be duplicated during a ship's normal working life.

Ships' design speeds are given, and, where known, speeds obtained during warship trials are also listed. These trial speeds are, of course, subject to the same qualifications as trial horsepower.

Thicknesses of armour are given in inches, rounded off to one decimal point. Only figures for armour on the most accessible parts of a ship have been listed, i.e., belt armour, control tower, large gun turrets and armoured deck.

Calibres of guns and torpedo tubes are in inches, rounded off to one decimal point unless stated. In the case of certain small calibre guns, the figures have been given in millimetres.

Wrecks lying in the approaches to the Flow in Hoy Sound and in Cantick Sound have been excluded from this account. The depths of water in which vessels lie, where given, are in metres, and because of the uneven nature of the sea-bed, are approximate.

20th October 1984   Stromness

. . . Nature seems to have given every degree of shelter to Scapa Flow that could possibly be expected in a roadstead of such extent; and therefore it wants no artificial shelter, a circumstance greatly in its favour . . .

. . . The depth of water is great, there being from 10-20 fathoms all over the Flow, the which in a confined Anchorage would be rather a disadvantage but as there is plenty of room here to stow the Anchor, I shall call it, in the Seaman's phrase, a Good fault . . .

. . . If we had a strong Fleet there in War time, it would prevent the enemy from going North-about Britain to Ireland or elsewhere should he ever attempt it. Our Fleet there would also intercept and prevent all the Enemy's Trade North-about Britain to Russia, Sweden, Norway, Denmark, Holland and Flanders, a route which those Nations often take, especially in War time . . .

from a Memorial submitted to the Lords Commissioners
of the Admiralty on 4th June, 1812 by Graeme Spence,
"late Maritime Surveyor to their Lordships."

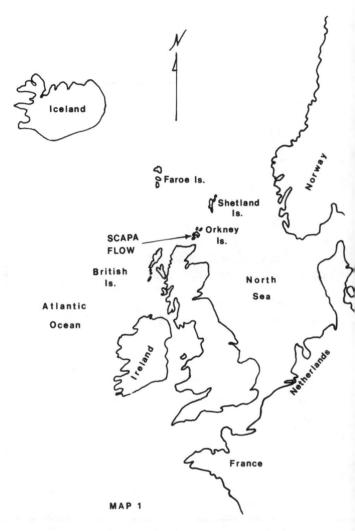

MAP 1

SCAPA FLOW'S STRATEGIC
POSITION IN NORTHERN EUROPE

0   200   400   600   800km.

HISTORICAL

(See Map 1)

Strategically situated as it is astride one of the main sea lanes to Europe, Scapa Flow in the Orkney Islands is located in a superbly commanding position. This has long been recognised — for example, a memorial addressed to the Lords Commissioners of the Admiralty in 1812, deals at length with the Flow's advantages as a naval base. It describes it as ". . . a Northern Roadstead in which a Fleet of Men of War might Rendezous and be ready to Act either on the offensive or defensive from this Advanced post as circumstances might require . . ."

However, it was not until just over a hundred years later that a formal British naval base organisation was established, following rapidly-deteriorating relations with Imperial Germany. In the space of some fifteen years that nation had become a major naval power in its own right, with a truly massive construction programme for all types of warship. At the outbreak of hostilities in August 1914, Scapa Flow's defence and shore facilities were very incomplete, with the anti-submarine barriers totally lacking. It was still possible for the *U18* to enter Scapa Flow by Hoxa Sound on the morning of 23rd November, 1914. Finding only a few destroyers and trawlers in the anchorages, she turned back through Hoxa Sound to look for more valuable targets, but her periscope had already been sighted by the examination steamer *Tokio*. The *U18* heard the sounds of the propellers of the searching vessels and stayed submerged, but with the sea-bed dangerous with scattered rocks and swirling currents, she was forced to put up her periscope from time to time, to find her way out. Eventually, she was rammed by the trawler *Dorothy Gray,* and the force of the blow damaged her hydroplane motor, as well as bending the periscope over at right angles. Unable to trim properly and without any means of observation, the *U18* tried to make for the open sea, but ran onto the Pentland Skerries. The crippled submarine was able to surface, and was then scuttled, with the captain and crew being picked up by the British destroyer *Garry.*

In fact, it was not until 1916 that the anti-submarine barriers were finally completed, and they included no less than 21 blockships that were sunk to close off Burra Sound and the eastern approaches through the Sounds between the Orcadian mainland and South Ronaldsay. The main entrances — Hoxa, Switha and Hoy Sounds — were guarded by boom defence nets, controlled minefields, and shore batteries of various calibres.

As is well known, the Flow acted as a base for elements of the British Grand Fleet throughout World War I, although various heavy units were detached to the Cromarty Firth and the Firth of Forth. On 9th July, 1917, the battleship *HMS Vanguard* blew up whilst at anchor off Flotta, sinking virtually immediately, with the loss of over 800 officers and men of her company. An official Inquiry found that the accident was caused by the detonation of unstable cordite in one of her magazines.

In the closing days of WWI, *UB116* tried to slip into the Flow through Hoxa Sound. She was picked up by detection equipment at the Quoyness observation station, and at 23.32 hours on 28th October, 1918 was blown up in the controlled minefield, some ¼ ml NE of Quoyness, Flotta. There were, not unexpectedly, no survivors from her crew of 36, and next day, to make doubly sure of her disposal, the sunken hulk was depth-charged. A quantity of oil and debris came to the surface, and her log was recovered by divers on 4th November.

In order to recover important papers such as code books, every effort was made by the Admiralty to locate and examine in detail remains of sunken German U-boats. Even at this stage in the war the German submarine campaign against Allied merchant shipping had been extremely active, only being called off on 20th October, 1918 when initial moves for an armistice were made by the government in Berlin.

Following the Armistice in November 1918, the major part of the German High Seas Fleet was interned in the Flow until the Versailles Peace Conference could decide on its fate. On the morning of 21st June, 1919, believing that some form of hostilities was about to be resumed, Rear-Admiral von Reuter, the officer commanding, gave the coded order for his ships to be scuttled. His move coincided with the departure of British guard ships on exercise for the day, and as a result 52 out of the 74 interned warships sank completely; the remaining 22 were beached or saved by Royal Naval boarding parties.

Salvage operations, first by Messrs Cox and Danks, and subsequently by Metal Industries Ltd, succeeded in raising the majority of the scuttled units by the beginning of World War II. However, for various reasons, three battleships and four cruisers still remain unsalvaged. The wrecks of not less than four of the scuttled destroyers also remain on the bottom of the Flow.

At the end of World War I, Scapa Flow's naval facilities were rapidly run down, most of the buildings and non-military equipment being sold off to private buyers. However, by 1938 it had become obvious that another war with Germany was almost inevitable, and work was accordingly put in hand to re-establish base facilities of all kinds. The work was much hampered by the Treasury severely restricting capital expenditure, this being especially so in the provision of adequate anti-submarine defences, particularly blockships.

On the night of 13th/14th October, 1939, a little over a month after the outbreak of World War II, the German submarine *U47*, under the command of Kapitänleutnant Günther Prien, slipped through a gap between blockships in Kirk Sound, and torpedoed the old battleship *HMS Royal Oak*. Hit hard, she capsized and sank in minutes, with the loss of over 800 of her complement, in one of the worst disasters in modern British naval history. This prompted a classic belated closing of the stable door, and no less than 20 additional blockships were subsequently scuttled to fill some of the more obvious gaps in the anti-submarine defences. To provide a permanent solution, the then First Lord of the Admiralty, Mr Winston Churchill, ordered the building of causeways to block totally Kirk, Skerry, East Weddel and Water Sounds, and these Churchill Barriers remain in use today as part of the local road system.

Having again given sterling service in World War II, naval base facilities were run down at the end of hostilities, but a limited presence was maintained until January 1957. In 1980 Orkney Islands Council acquired the remaining Lyness facilities from the Ministry of Defence.

GENERAL DESCRIPTION OF SCAPA FLOW

(See Map 2)

The "North Sea Pilot" describes Scapa Flow as an inland sea. About 80 square miles in area, it is enclosed by the Mainland and South Isles of Orkney. With depths averaging 20 metres and rarely in excess of 60 metres, as well as good holding ground, it provides a magnificent natural anchorage. Tidal streams, although strong in the Hoxa and Hoy Sound entrances, are within the Flow itself slight. Vessels of all sizes can find safe shelter in every weather condition; however, local geography is such that the fetch is sufficient for considerable sea states to occur during very stormy weather.

In addition to the 80-odd charted wrecks, the Flow's bed is littered with old cables of every kind, twisted remains of anti-submarine nets, and associated debris of wartime vintage. The bottom is mainly composed of soft silts which are easily stirred up, seriously impairing visibility, and underwater visual distances also vary according to the location and time of year. Burra Sound, for example, with a strong tidal flow and no silt, has a typical visibility of 60 to 70 feet. This may, however, be seriously reduced by plankton "bloom" in May and September. Ashore, the remains of naval and military installations still litter the landscape. The most imposing of those remaining are the "Golden Wharf" and one of the oil fuel storage tanks at Lyness.

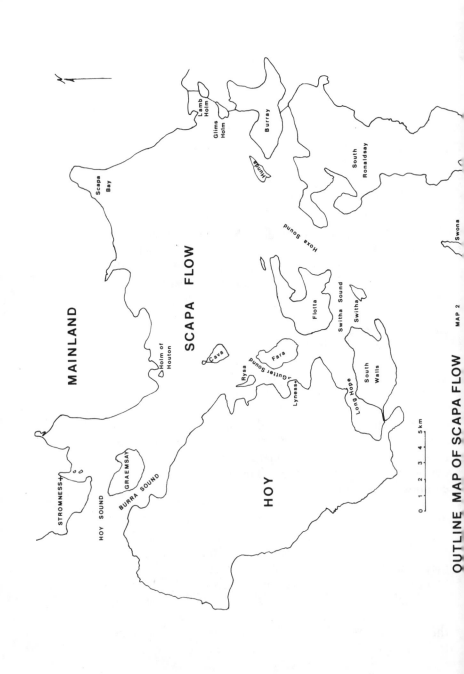

OUTLINE MAP OF SCAPA FLOW   MAP 2

DIVING AND SHIPPING MOVEMENTS

Diving in the Scapa Flow area, along with the movement of shipping, is covered by the Orkney Harbour Areas Byelaws, and the attention of those wishing to dive in the Flow is particularly drawn to Byelaw 33:

(1) No person who is wearing or equipped with clothes or apparatus designed or adapted for swimming underwater or diving shall swim underwater, dive or fish in a harbour area except with the written permission of the Harbour Master.

(2) Without prejudice to the foregoing provisions of this byelaw, no person shall swim underwater, dive, or fish

    (a) within 100 metres of any of Her Majesty's ships or vessels, including the wrecks of any such ships or vessels, within a harbour area, save with the licence in writing of the Queen's Harbourmaster, Rosyth, and in accordance with any conditions attached thereto; nor

    (b) within 30 metres of the walls, slipways, or boundaries of Her Majesty's Royal Naval Oil Fuel Depot, Lyness.

In addition, a Diving Permit issued by the Director of Harbours must be obtained by those intending to dive in the Orkney Harbour Areas (Wide Firth/Shapinsay Sound, and Scapa Flow).

Divers are also *reminded* that the *nearest emergency decompression* facilities are located in Aberdeen. In the event of a *diving incident requiring medical attention,* telephone Kirkwall 2763, or 999.

Unauthorised removal of fittings from the wrecks is illegal, and if unchecked could lead to the wholesale destruction of a unique attraction. Divers are therefore strongly requested to refrain from "souvenir-hunting."

GENERAL DESCRIPTION
OF WRECKS

(See also Table 1)

The condition of wrecks varies from the fragmentary (*Lycia* at No. 2 Barrier, Skerry Sound) to the complete (*Dresden*, east of Cava). Those exposed to the full force of tide and weather (such as the blockships) have by and large suffered the most damage, and are commonly broken into several pieces. Likewise — due to the massive internal ammunition explosion — the remains of *HMS Vanguard* cover a large area of sea-bed to the north of Flotta. Salvage work on some of the seven largest remaining scuttled German warships has resulted in considerable damage to otherwise intact hulls. Attempts (during 1975) to remove a live torpedo from the more or less complete remains of *UB116* in Hoxa Sound by means of a small explosive charge resulted in the detonation of the main warhead, and the consequent wrecking of the hull. Because of their light construction, the hulls of the beached or stranded German WWI destroyers have suffered major storm damage.

Of the 80 or so charted wrecks in the Flow, by far the largest group are the blockships, sunk as part of the anti-submarine defences. There are a total of 43 altogether, 21 sunk during WWI and the remaining 22 during WWII. Eleven or twelve have seemingly been salvaged at various times since then, but no accurate details exist. The best known wrecks are obviously those of the German warships of the High Seas Fleet, scuttled on 21st June, 1919. Although most were subsequently salvaged during a long-term operation (during the 1920's and 30's), three battleships, four cruisers, and not less than four destroyers remain. The total of German naval wrecks is completed by a U-boat, an escort vessel and an E-boat, sunk separately at other times.

There are nine Royal Naval wrecks: two battleships, one fleet minesweeper, one trawler, two M.F.V.s, two tugs and four drifters. A miscellaneous group of 14 other vessels includes a WWI oiler, a trawler and a concrete barge.

The list of charted wrecks is, however, almost certainly a minimum figure, as earlier and smaller casualties have probably disintegrated or sunk deeply into the silts which cover so much of the bottom of the Flow.

Ownership of the various wrecks (where known) is summarised in Table 2.

TABLE 1
Classes of Wrecks

Type	No.	Remarks
Blockships	7*	Burra Sound
Blockships	36*	Churchill Barriers
German Naval	14	Mainly N and E of Cava
British Naval	12	—
Miscellaneous	14	Mostly unknown
	83	

* Includes 12 blockships subsequently salvaged or removed.

Diver in the hold of barge *YC21* investigating the
twin anti-aircraft guns salvaged from *F2*.

Centrifugal window on the bridge of one of the German ships.

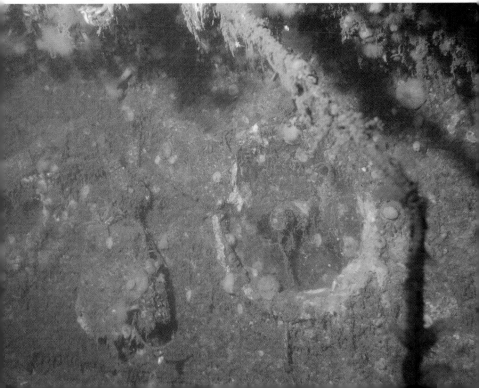

A mooring cleat on *SMS Brummer*.

Sea Anemone.

Diver exploring the wreck of *SMS Brummer*.

TABLE 2
Wreck Ownership

Name	Owner
HMS Vanguard	M.O.D. (N.)
HMS Royal Oak	M.O.D. (N.)
HMS Roedean	D. Spence, Stromness
HM ships Oceana, Strathgary, *Alexandra II, Dewey Eve,* *Imbat, Token, Catherine,* *Ruby, Legend*	M.O.D. (N.)
Prudentia	?M.O.D. (N.)
Blockships (Churchill Barriers)	M.O.D. (N.)
Blockships (Burra Sound)	M.O.D. (N.)
SMS Kronprinz Wilhelm	Clark Diving Services Ltd., Lerwick
SMS Markgraf	Clark Diving Services Ltd., Lerwick
SMS König	Clark Diving Services Ltd., Lerwick
SMS Karlsruhe	Clark Diving Services Ltd., Lerwick
SMS Dresden	M.O.D. (N.) Leased by Clark Diving
SMS Brummer	M.O.D. (N.) Leased by Clark Diving
SMS Cöln	M.O.D. (N.) Leased by Clark Diving
F2	?M.O.D. (N.)
UB116	D. Spence, Stromness
E Boat	?M.O.D. (N.)
Var. German Destroyers	?M.O.D. (N.)

DETAILED DESCRIPTION
OF WRECKS

1. THE BLOCKSHIPS (See Table 3 and Maps 3 and 4)

The blockships comprise a remarkably varied group, ranging in size from the 8900-ton *Inverlane* to the *Gondolier* of 173 tons. Most were specifically bought by the Admiralty as blockships, but a few were war casualties, damaged beyond repair. The *Gondolier* is, in fact, the oldest, built in 1866. This little paddle-ship sailed on the Caledonian Canal as an excursion steamer for over 70 years, before being sold to the Admiralty in 1939.

At least one of the blockships was a war prize. The *Empire Seaman*, ex *Morea*, a German steamer, was seized in the Bay of Biscay by the Royal Navy in 1940, while she was trying to slip back to Germany through the British blockade.

One of the more unusual vessels is the *Collingdoc*, a Great Lakes steamer, beached at the extreme south end of No. 4 Barrier on South Ronaldsay. She exhibits the very characteristic features of 'Lakers', a long narrow hull with the engine and funnel aft and the bridge right forward in the eyes of the ship. Her bridge is still protected by the remains of a primitive armour of concrete slabs.

The *Gobernador Bories*, ex *Wordsworth*, was owned by a Chilean whaling company, the Sociedad Anonima Ballenera de Magellanes, and registered in Punta Arenas. The *A.C.6* and the *F/C Pontoon* were salvage equipment originally used by Metal Industries Ltd.

Of the 43 blockships sunk, 11 or possibly 12 were subsequently salvaged. The *Tabarka*, originally sunk in 1941 in Kirk Sound, was raised in 1944 and re-sunk in

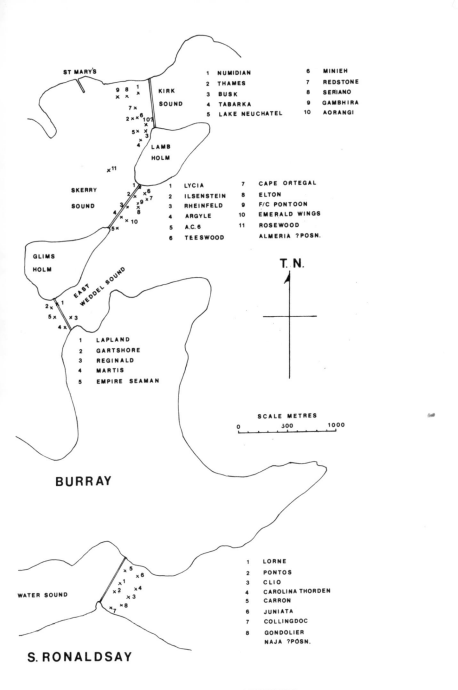

KIRK SOUND

1 NUMIDIAN	6 MINIEH
2 THAMES	7 REDSTONE
3 BUSK	8 SERIANO
4 TABARKA	9 GAMBHIRA
5 LAKE NEUCHATEL	10 AORANGI

ST MARY'S

LAMB HOLM

SKERRY SOUND

1 LYCIA	7 CAPE ORTEGAL
2 ILSENSTEIN	8 ELTON
3 RHEINFELD	9 F/C PONTOON
4 ARGYLE	10 EMERALD WINGS
5 A.C.6	11 ROSEWOOD
6 TEESWOOD	ALMERIA ?POSN.

GLIMS HOLM

EAST WEDDEL SOUND

T. N.

1	LAPLAND
2	GARTSHORE
3	REGINALD
4	MARTIS
5	EMPIRE SEAMAN

SCALE METRES

0   300   1000

BURRAY

WATER SOUND

1	LORNE
2	PONTOS
3	CLIO
4	CAROLINA THORDEN
5	CARRON
6	JUNIATA
7	COLLINGDOC
8	GONDOLIER
	NAJA ?POSN.

S. RONALDSAY

THE CHURCHILL BARRIER BLOCKSHIPS. MAP 3

Burra Sound. There is no trace of her in up-to-date wreck listings, so it appears that she was later salvaged and removed.

Little remains visible today of the one hundred thousand gross tons of shipping sunk as blockships in two World Wars. The bows of the *Inverlane,* with the foremast still standing, lie in Burra Sound, well exposed above high water. Given the terrible winter conditions which she has had to withstand, it is a tribute to her builders that she has lasted so long.

In Kirk Sound, nothing is to be seen above water of the ten blockships which once closed this entry to Scapa Flow. At the time of the sinking of the *Royal Oak,* there were only three blockships there: the *Minieh,* the *Thames,* and, to the north of them, the *Seriano.* The route of the *U47* into Scapa Flow was to the north of the *Seriano,* going close to the shore. On her way back out to the open sea, the submarine took the other side of the channel, going to the south of the *Thames.*

In Skerry Sound, something more of the original blockships can be seen. The remains of the *Lycia,* cut down to engine-room level, lie alongside the extreme north-east end of No. 2 Barrier. A crane barge, marked on the charts as *F/C Pontoon,* is still substantially intact with her mooring winches showing, in the middle of the Sound. The barge is little more than a floating steel box. Just to the north-east of it, the remains of the *Cape Ortegal* and the *Elton,* much broken up, can be seen at low water.

At No. 3 Barrier, East Weddel Sound, the most prominent blockship is the *Reginald,* lying at the south-east end. The remains of this iron ship, with her schooner stern lying on her starboard side, are well exposed at high water. Of the *Empire Seaman* and *Martis,* little is now visible except a few bent sections of plate showing above high water.

The remains of three blockships are still to be seen above high water in Water Sound. All are to be found on the east side of No. 4 Barrier. The hulk of the *Carron,* lying approximately north-south, is beached at

T.N.

GRAEMSAY

HOY

BAY
OF
CREEKLAND

MONESS
PIER

1 BUDRIE.
2 INVERLANE.
3 MOYLE.
4 GOBERNADOR BORIES.
5 URMSTONE GRANGE.
6 ROTHERFIELD.
7 RONDA.

SCALE METRES

0   500   1000

BURRA SOUND BLOCKSHIPS. MAP 4

the Burray end of the barrier. Although her hull is substantially intact, the superstructure has almost disappeared, and the stern mast has collapsed across the hull. The remains of the *Pontos* can still be seen, roughly in the middle of Water Sound, with the forward section of the hull and a davit aft showing above high water.

With her concrete-lined bridge and bow section buried in the beach at the extreme south-east end of No. 4 Barrier, the former Great Lakes steamer *Collingdoc* is the most accessible of the blockships.

TABLE 3

Blockships

Kirk Sound (No. 1 Barrier)

Name	Date Sunk	Gross Tons	Notes
Aorangi	WW1	4268	Steel single-screw steamer, built 1883 Glasgow. Registered Dunedin, New Zealand. Raised by East Coast Wrecking Co. 8/9/20, and re-sunk off Holm Kirkyard.
Busk	1940	367	Steel single-screw steamer, built 1906 North Shields. Registered Whitehaven, Cumberland. Broke up during gale.
Gambhira (ex *War Merlin*)	1939	5257	Steel single-screw steamer, built 1910 Sunderland. Registered London. Salvaged 1943 and used in Liverpool Bay as ASDIC target. Finally sunk off Llandudno, N. Wales.
Lake Neuchatel (ex *Renfrew*, ex *Claveresk*, ex *Houstone*, ex *Mari* ex *Ulversmead*)	1939	3859	Steel single-screw steamer, built 1907 Sunderland. Registered London. Salvaged 1948 by Metal Industries Ltd.

Minieh	1915	2890	Iron single-screw steamer, built
(ex Alsatia)			1876 Glasgow. Registered London. Hull removed.
Numidian	WW1	4836	Steel single-screw steamer, built 1891 Glasgow. Registered Glasgow. Salvaged February 1924 by East Coast Salvage Co.
Redstone	1940	3110	Steel single-screw steamer, built
(ex Margari,			1918 W. Hartlepool. Registered
ex Orbe,			London. Removed.
ex Wye Crag,			
ex War Crag)			
Seriano	1939	3543	Steel single-screw steamer, built
(ex Evansville,			1917 Michigan. Registered Monte-
ex Lake Tahoe,			video, Uruguay. Removed.
ex SNA 4)			
Tabarka	1941	2624	Steel single-screw steamer, built
(ex Pollux)			1909 Rotterdam. Registered Rouen. French, seized Falmouth July 1940. Raised and removed to Burra Sound 27/7/44.
Thames	1914	1327	Steel single-screw steamer, built 1887 Glasgow. Registered Grangemouth. Stern removed. Hull cut down to level of main deck.

Skerry Sound (No. 2 Barrier)

Name	Date Sunk	Gross Tons	Notes
A.C. 6 (Barge)	1941	—	Ex Metal Industries Ltd. Broken up.
Almeria	1915	2418	Steel single-screw steamer, built
(ex Wakefield)			1888 Sunderland. Registered Cardiff. Originally purchased as accommodation ship.
Argyle	1914	1185	Iron single-screw steamer, built 1872 Hull. Registered Hull. Much broken up.
Cape Ortegal	1939	4896	Steel single-screw steamer, built 1911 Glasgow. Registered Glasgow. Rolled over and broke up during gale.
Elton	1915	2461	Steel single-screw steamer, built 1880 W. Hartlepool. Registered W. Hartlepool. Midships section with engine remains.

Name	Date Sunk	Gross Tons	Notes
Emerald Wings (ex *Nicolaos Baikos*, ex *Deputé Pierre Goujon*)	1940	2139	Steel single-screw steamer, built 1920 Cherbourg. Registered London. Much broken up.
F/C Pontoon	1941	—	Ex Metal Industries Ltd.
Ilsenstein	1940	1508	Steel single-screw steamer, built 1898 Kiel. Registered Bremen. Replaced *Cape Ortegal*.
Lycia	1940	2338	Steel single-screw motorship, built 1924 Port Glasgow. Registered Glasgow. Hull cut down to engine-room level. Lies against N. end of No. 2 Barrier.
Rheinfeld (ex *Ramses*)	1914	3634	Steel single-screw steamer, built 1893 Newcastle. Registered Hamburg. Much broken up. Lies beside wreck of *Elton*.
Rosewood (ex *Blakemoor*)	1915	1757	Steel single-screw steamer, built 1889 S. Shields. Registered S. Shields. Displaced to west of Lamb Holm. Almost completely dispersed.
Teeswood (ex *Westwood*)	1914	1589	Built 1882. Only engines remain.

East Weddel Sound (No. 3 Barrier)

Name	Date Sunk	Gross Tons	Notes
Empire Seaman (ex *Morea*)	1940	1921	Steel single-screw steamer, built 1922 Lübeck. Registered London. War prize. Seized by Royal Navy 1940. Bow and stern cut off. Engines removed. Midships section broken up.
Gartshore	1915	1564	Iron single-screw steamer, built 1880 S. Shields and registered there. No trace of wreck.
Lapland (ex *Dauntless*, ex *Ptarmigan*)	1915	1234	Steel single-screw steamer, built 1890 Dundee. Registered Liverpool. Totally collapsed, directly beneath barrier.
Martis (ex *William Balls*)	1940	2483	Steel single-screw steamer, built 1894 S. Shields. Registered London. Stern and bows removed.

| Reginald | 1915 | 930 | Iron 3-masted motor schooner, built 1878 Glasgow and registered there. Stern section lying on its side shows characteristic schooner shape. |

Water Sound (No. 4 Barrier)

Name	Date Sunk	Gross Tons	Notes
Carolina Thorden	1942	3645	Steel single-screw motor tanker, built 1938 Sweden. Registered Helsinki. Strengthened for ice. Bombed and burnt off Faroes. Sunk to replace *Gondolier*. Apparently mostly removed.
Carron (ex *Glasgow*)	1940	1017	Steel single-screw steamer, built 1894 Dundee. Registered Grangemouth. Freighter belonging to Carron Iron Co. of Falkirk. Mast collapsed and lying across hull.
Clio	1914	2733	Steel single-screw steamer, built 1889 Hartelpool. Registered Hull. Boilers and engines exposed.
Collingdoc (ex *D. B. Hanna*)	1942	1780	Steel single-screw Great Lakes steamer, built 1925 Hill-on-Tees. Registered Fort William, Ontario, Canada.
Gondolier	1940	173	Iron paddle-steamer, built 1866 Glasgow. Registered Glasgow. Ex David MacBrayne Ltd., Caledonian Canal Service. Rolled over and sank in deep water.
Juniata (ex *Sprucol*)	1940	1139	Steel twin-screw motor tanker. Built 1918 Sunderland. Registered London.
Lorne	1915	1186	Iron single-screw steamer, built 1873 Hull. Registered Southampton. Broken up. Part of hull lying to east of *Clio*. Partially dispersed by explosives.
Naja	1939	—	Concrete barge. Formerly owned by Jas. Anderson, Stromness. Sunk immediately north of *Clio*.

inald off No. 3 Barrier   D

Pontos	1914	2265	Steel single-screw steamer, built
(ex St John City,			1891 Glasgow. Registered Andros,
ex *Clan Macnab)*			Greece.

Burra Sound

Name	Date Sunk	Gross Tons	Notes
Budrie	1915	2252	Steel single-screw steamer, built
(ex Cannig,			1882 Glasgow. Registered Bombay.
ex *Golconda)*			
Gobernador Bories	1915	2332	Iron single-screw steamer, built
(ex Wordsworth)			1882 W. Hartlepool. Registered
			Punta Arenas, Chile. Hull broken
			up, stern intact.
Inverlane	1944	8900	Steel single-screw motor tanker,
			built 1938 Vegesack, near Bremen.
			Registered Dublin. Hull exposed 50
			feet at high water. Only midships
			and bow remain. Mined off S.
			Shields 1939.
Moyle	1940	1761	Steel single-screw steamer, built
			1907 Troon. Registered Belfast.
Rotherfield	1914	2831	Steel single-screw steamer, built
			1889 W. Hartlepool. Registered
			London. Wreck blown up and dis-
			persed 1962.
Ronda	1915	1941	Steel single-screw steamer, built
(ex Rydal Holme)			1889 Sunderland. Registered Hull.
			Wreck blown up and dispersed
			1962.
Urmstone Grange	1914	3423	Steel single-screw steamer, built
			1894 Belfast. Registered London.
			Wreck blown up and dispersed
			1962.

2. NAVAL WRECKS (See Tables 4 and 5 and Map 5)

In all, the remains of 14 German warships lie in Scapa Flow, ranging in size from the 25,000 ton *König* class battleships to the submarine *UB116* of 516 tons. With the exception of the *F2*, a WWII *Geleitboote* (fast escort vessel), and possibly an E-boat (MTB), all date from WWI. They are now the last remaining examples of warships dating from an era when the naval balance of power was all-important, prior to the entry of aircraft into the military equation.

The scuttling of the German High Seas Fleet in June 1919 effectively, albeit somewhat abruptly, solved some extremely vexed diplomatic problems, and made the signing of the eventual Peace Treaty that much easier. Principal concern over the interned warships was their eventual disposal, there being acute alarm in Whitehall that the possible redistribution of a large fleet of modern, well-constructed and battle-tried vessels could seriously affect the then current British naval predominance. Coupled to this were extreme domestic financial pressures which rendered vital a speedy reduction in the country's maritime strength to more acceptable peace-time levels.

Of the 74 German warships involved in the 1919 scuttling operation, 22 were beached by the Royal Navy, and later salvaged. The bulk of the remainder were initially raised by Cox and Danks and subsequently by Metal Industries Ltd. The latter's activities finished with uncanny timing just prior to the outbreak of WWII in September 1939. Post-WWII salvage was confined to the piecemeal removal of heavy armour plate and non-ferrous metal, and no ships were raised complete. At the end of these operations there still remained the wrecks of three battleships, four light cruisers, and not less than four destroyers.

Of the 50 destroyers scuttled in June 1919, 19 were salvaged by the Royal Navy. One of these, the *S54*, was driven ashore on Flotta in February 1920, whilst being towed south, and became a total loss. The *V83* was stripped where she lay on Rysa Little, by Cox and

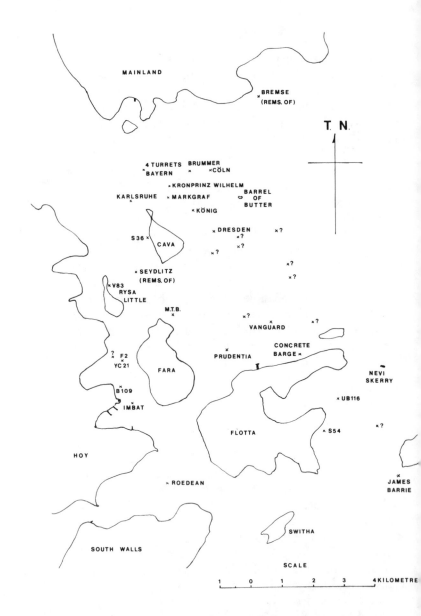

THE WRECKS OF CENTRAL SCAPA FLOW. MAP 5

Danks. After being used in the raising of the *Hindenburg*, the gutted hulk of the *S36* was run ashore on the western side of Fara. Rather confusingly, this is also where the cruiser *Nürnberg* was successfully beached by the R.N. in 1919, but she was definitely refloated and towed to the Forth for breaking-up in 1920. The remains of an unknown German destroyer variously referred to as the *B109*, the *S69* and the *G69*, lie 4.2 cables due south of the F2 buoy.

The *G89* was salvaged in 1922 by the Stromness Salvage Syndicate, and after being stripped, was used by Cox and Danks during the raising of the *Seydlitz*. Four more destroyers were raised in 1924 by the Scapa Flow Salvage Co., and were taken away for breaking-up.

The only positively-identified WWII German Naval wreck is the *F2*, which sank in Gutter Sound on 30th December, 1946. A *Geleitboote* approximates to a small British escort destroyer, and her position 1 ml north of the Golden Wharf is marked by a red can buoy. The circumstances of her sinking are not definitely known but she may have been used for trials of some kind and sunk on their completion. The *F2* and other members of her class served essentially as experimental ships. Their sophisticated machinery gave so much trouble that they never became operational in their intended role. In addition they were poor sea-boats. A wreck listed as a German E-boat (MTB) lies off the north side of Fara, close to where the *V78* sank in 1919, but the latter was salvaged in 1925. The remains of the E-boat's hull, much broken up, lie in 10 metres of water, and no information as to her identity or sinking is available.

TABLE 4: German Naval Wrecks

Name/No.	Type	Tonnage	Date Sunk	Position	Water Depths (m)	Notes
SMS König	Battleship	25,388	21/6/19	¾ ml NE of Cava	40	Scuttled
SMS Markgraf	Battleship	25,388	21/6/19	½ ml NE of Calf of Cava	46	Scuttled
SMS Kronprinz Wilhelm	Battleship	25,388	21/6/19	¾ ml NE of Calf of Cava	34	Scuttled
SMS Cöln	Light Cruiser	5,531	21/6/19	1¾ ml NE of Calf of Cava	34	Scuttled
SMS Brummer	Light Cruiser	4,308	21/6/19	1 ml NE of Calf of Cava	34	Scuttled
SMS Karlsruhe	Light Cruiser	5,354	21/6/19	½ ml W of Calf of Cava	24	Scuttled
SMS Dresden	Light Cruiser	5,531	21/6/19	¾ ml E of Cava	34	Scuttled
S36	Torpedo Boat/ Destroyer	789	?1928/29	W side of Cava, North Ho.	4	Scuttled, salvaged, beached
S54	Torpedo Boat/ Destroyer	902	12/2/20	¾ ml S of Quoyness, Flotta	16	Scuttled, salvaged, wrecked
V83	Torpedo Boat/ Destroyer	909	21/6/19	E side of Rysa Little	8-20	Scuttled, beached
Unknown	Torpedo Boat/ Destroyer	?	?1926	4.3 cables S of F2 Buoy	10	Scuttled, salvaged, re-sunk
—	E Boat (MTB)	—	Not known	N end of Fara	10	?
UB116	Submarine	516	28/10/18	Pan Hope ENE of Quoyness	25	Blown up by controlled mine
F2	Escort Vessel	756	30/12/46	Gutter Sound off Rysa Lodge	18	Sunk (? Trials)

TABLE 5: Royal Naval Wrecks

Name	Type	Tonnage	Date Sunk	Position	Water Depth (m)	Notes
HMS Royal Oak	Battleship	29,150	14/10/39	1 ml S of Scapa Pier	26	Torpedoed
HMS Vanguard	Battleship	19,560	9/7/17	1 nm NNE Flotta Terminal	34	Magazine explosion
HMS Roedean	Fleet M/S	1,094	13/1/15	Entrance to Longhope	15	? Fouled ram *HMS Imperieuse*? Mined?
HM Tug Oceana	Tug (A.B.V.)	337	19/10/18	"At Scapa"	—	Lost by collision
HM Trawler Strathgary	Trawler (B.D.V.)	202	6/7/15	"Sunk off Scapa"	—	Lost by collision
HM Tug Alexandra II	Tug	168	28/10/15	Hoxa Sound	—	Wrecked
HM Drifter Dewey Eve	M/SW Drifter	109	9/6/40	"304° No. 6 Buoy, distant 1 cable"	15	Lost by collision
HM Drifter Imbat	Drifter	92	4/2/41	300m E of Lyness Pier	14	Lost by collision
HM Drifter Token	Aux. Pat. Drifter	89	23/12/41	Skerry Sound	—	Grounded and wrecked
HM Drifter Catherine	Aux. Pat. Drifter	78	8/6/42	Not known	—	Foundered
HM Drifter Ruby	Ferry ? (M.F.V.)	46	5/10/42	Lamb Holm	—	Wrecked in gale
HM Drifter Legend	?M.F.V.	—	28/12/42	Flotta	—	Wrecked

Details of size, armament, condition, etc., of the German wrecks are listed below, together with photographs and line drawings where available.

BATTLESHIPS: *SMS KÖNIG, KRONPRINZ WILHELM,*
MARKGRAF — KÖNIG class

Displacement	25,388 tons
Dimensions	575.5 × 96.8 × 30.2 feet
Machinery	3 sets of turbines driving 3 propellers
	Coal/Oil Fired
Trials	*König* 43,000 SHP = 21 kts.
	Kronprinz
	Wilhelm 46,200 SHP = 21.3 kts.
	Markgraf 41,400 SHP = 21 kts.
Armour	Main belt 13.8″, armour deck 3.9″,
	turrets 11.8″, control tower (fore) 11.8″,
	(aft) 7.9″
Armament	10 - 12″ (5 × 2), 14 - 5.9″,
	6 (finally 0) - 3.45″, 4 (finally 2) - 3.45″ A.A.
	guns,
	5 - 19.7″ submerged T.T. (1 bow, 4 beam)
Complement	1,136 officers and men
Builders/completion dates	*König* Kaiserliches Werft 10.8.14
	Wilhelmshaven
	Kronprinz Germaniawerft 8.11.14
	Wilhelm Kiel
	Markgraf A. G. Weser 1.10.14
	Bremen

Condition of Wrecks:

König — Capsized. Lying with starboard side maindeck on bottom. Hull blown open with many sharp edges. Much indistinguishable wreckage. Water depth 40m. Silty bottom. Visibility (June) 30 feet. Upper works buried in silt.

Markgraf — Capsized. Hole blasted into engine-room. Remainder of hull intact. Water depth 46m. Bottom sand and silt. Parts of main deck clear of sea-bed.

Kronprinz Wilhelm — Resting on sea-bed keel up, with starboard-side maindeck on bottom. Considerable damage to hull in areas of boiler-rooms and engine-rooms. Flat-bottom hull with four prominent bilge-keels. Port-side covered with rich marine plant-growth. Water depth 34m. Visibility (September) 50 feet.

SMS Markgr

Aorar

THE "AORANGI" ASHORE IN HOLM SOUND 27-9-20 T KENT

COPYRIGHT ABRAHAMS 1064   GERMAN BATTLESHIP "KRONPRINZ WILHELM"   DEVONPORT

SURRENDERING AT SCAPA FLOW NOVEMBER 21ST. 1918

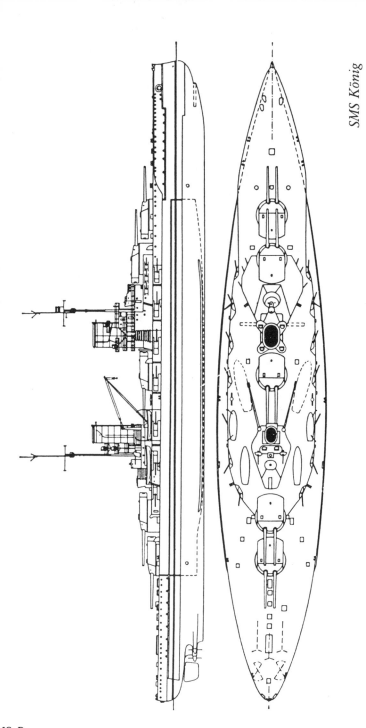

SMS König

MS Brummer

MS Kronprinz Wilhelm

FAST MINE-LAYING CRUISER: *SMS BRUMMER*

— BREMSE class

Displacement	4,308 tons
Dimensions	461.7 × 44.3 × 19.7 feet
Machinery	2 sets turbines driving 2 propellers
	Coal/Oil Fired
	33,000 SHP = 28 kts. (design)
	42,797 SHP = 28 kts. (trial)
Armour	Belt 1.6″, armour deck 0.6″ control tower 3.9″
Armament	4 - 5.9″, 2 - 3.4″ A.A. guns
Complement	309 officers and men
Builders	A. G. Vulcan, Stettin. Completed 1916.

Condition of Wreck

Resting on starboard side. In very good condition overall. Mast rests on sea-bed, with antenna, rangefinder and lamps still in place. Main deck-gun on bow in very good condition. Both anchor-chains are run out and hang over the starboard bow. Hole in port bow, and large hole in port side of hull. Propellers missing. Water depth 34m.

SMS Brummer

LIGHT CRUISERS: *SMS DRESDEN* and *CÖLN*

— DRESDEN (II) class

Displacement	5,531 tons
Dimensions	510.2 × 46.9 × 21.1 feet
Machinery	2 sets of turbines driving 2 propellers
	Coal/Oil Fired
	31,000 SHP = 27.5 kts. (design)
Trials	*Dresden* 49,428 SHP = 27.8 kts.
	Cöln 48,708 SHP = 29.3 kts.
Armour	Main belt 2.4″, deck 2.4″, control tower 3.9″
Armament	8 - 5.9″, 3 - 3.4″ A.A. guns (in 1918 only 2),
	4 - 23.6″ deck TT, 200 mines
Complement	559 officers and men
Builders/com-	*Dresden* Howaldtswerke 1918
pletion dates	Kiel
	Cöln Blohm & Voss 1918
	Hamburg

Condition of Wrecks

Dresden — Resting on port side, and in very good condition. Mainmast still intact. Upper decks show signs of slight damage. Starboard anchor-chain run out and lying on sea-bed, port anchor-chain not to be seen. Wreck covered with rich marine growth. Depth 34m.

Cöln — Lying on starboard side, and almost completely intact, apart from propellers and anchor missing. Impressive rudders. Water depth 34m. Silty bottom.

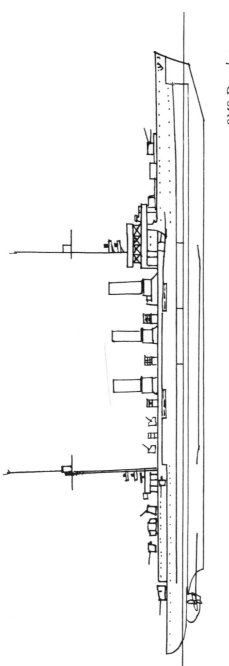

SMS Dresden

LIGHT CRUISER: *SMS KARLSRUHE* – KÖNIGSBERG (II) class

Displacement	5,354 tons
Dimensions	496.7 × 46.9 × 20.7 feet
Machinery	2 sets of turbines driving 2 propellers
	Coal/Oil Fired
	31,000 SHP = 27.5 kts. (design)
	55,700 SHP = 27.7 kts. (trial)
Armour	Main belt 2.4", deck 2.4", control tower 3.9"
Armament	8 - 5.9", 2 - 3.5" A.A. guns,
	2 - 19.7" deck TT, 200 mines
Complement	475 officers and men
Builders	Kaiserliches Werft, Wilhelmshaven.
	Completed 1916

Condition of Wreck

Lying on starboard side. Heavily damaged, with midships and forward section blasted open, and only the stern section intact. Forward gun-turret resting on sea-bed. Fire control tower ripped out of deck and lying on sea-bed, as are masts. Starboard anchor-chain run out and also lying on bottom. Water depth 24m.

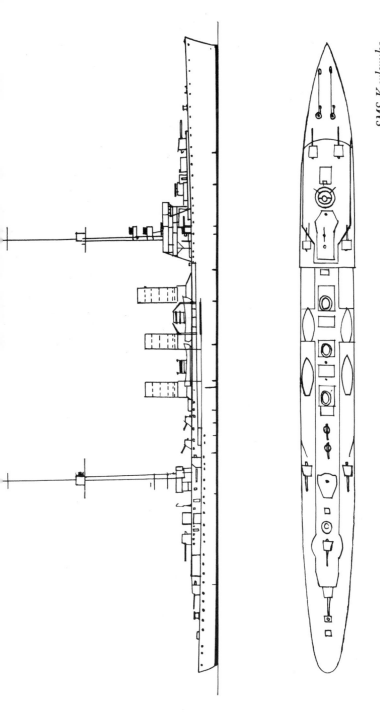

SMS Karlsruhe

TORPEDO BOAT/DESTROYERS: *S36* — Class S31-36

Displacement	789 tons
Dimensions	261.2 × 27.3 × 11.9 feet
Machinery	2 sets of turbines driving 2 propellers
	Oil-fired
	24,000 SHP = 33.5 kts. (design)
	23,516 SHP = 34.2 kts. (trial)
Armament	3 - 3.4″ guns, 6 - 19.7″ deck T.T.
	(2 × 2, 2 × 1), 24 mines
Complement	83 officers and men
Builders	Germaniawerft, Kiel. Completed 1916

V83 — Class V67-84

Displacement	909 tons
Dimensions	269.0 × 27.3 × 12.8 feet
Machinery	2 sets of turbines driving 2 propellers
	Oil-fired
	23,500 SHP = 34.0 kts. (design)
	24,400 SHP = 36.6 kts. (trial)
Armament	3 - 3.4″ guns, 6 - 19.7″ deck T.T.
	(2 × 2, 2 × 1), 24 mines
Complement	87 officers and men
Builders	A. G. Vulcan, Hamburg. Completed 1916

S54 — Class S53-66

Displacement	902 tons
Dimensions	272.6 × 27.4 × 12.8 feet
Machinery	2 sets of turbines driving 2 propellers
	Oil-fired
	24,000 SHP = 34.0 kts. (design)
	25,900 SHP = 35.1 kts. (trial)
Armament	3 - 4.1″ guns, 6 - 19.7″ deck T.T.
	(2 × 2, 2 × 1), 24 mines
Complement	87 officers and men
Builders	Schichau, Elbing. Completed 1916

Condition of Wrecks

S36 — Lies in shallow water adjacent to North House, Cava. Only the bow section (in poor condition) now remains.

V83 — Her position on the east side of Rysa Little is as shown in the official report completed after her beaching by the R.N. An unsuccessful attempt was made by Cox and Danks to raise her in 1926. Now lying upright on her keel, but broken in half, with the bow in 8m of water and the stern in 20m. Stern in good condition. Gun lying on port side of ship. Hull surrounded by wreckage.

S54 — Beached by R.N. salvage parties on Fara. A picture

German destroyers in Scapa Fl[

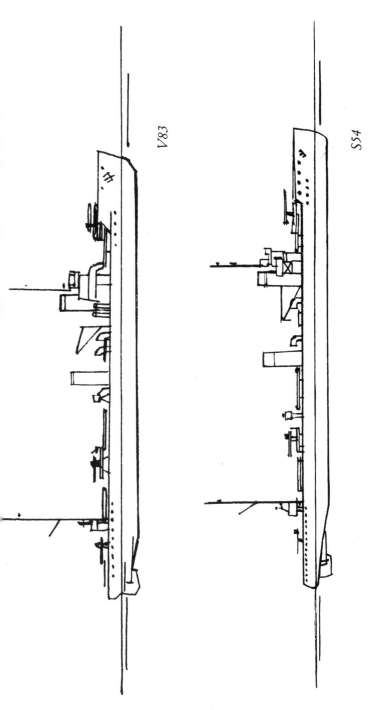

V83

S54

in Stromness Museum display

E

taken in October 1919 shows the vessel lying at anchor off Longhope along with other salvaged warships. In February 1920 she was driven ashore on the east side of Flotta while being towed away for breaking up. Cox and Danks made an unsuccessful attempt to raise her on 20th October, 1931. The hull was blown open during subsequent salvage operations and much damaged by storms. It now lies in 16m of water.

Unknown Destroyer — *?G109* — Bow and stern removed. Midsection lying on port side in 15m of water.

COASTAL SUBMARINE: *UB116* — Class UB111

Displacement	516 tons (surface)
	651 tons (submerged)
Dimensions	181.4 × 19.0 × 12.1 feet
Machinery	2 six-cylinder AEG diesel/electric motors driving 2 propellers
	1100 SHP = 13.6 kts. (design surface)
	788 SHP = kts. (design submerged)
Armament	5 - 19.7" T.T. (4 bow, 1 stern), 1 - 4.1" gun
Complement	34 officers and men
Built	Blohm & Voss, Hamburg. Completed 1918

Condition of Wreck

Blown to pieces in 1975 during an attempt to remove a live torpedo. Water depth 26m. According to the Hydrographic Department she was raised in 1919 but re-sunk in her present position. Bottom: soft sand into which most of the remains have sunk.

UB116

ENG. RM. | ACCOM. | CONTROL ROOM | ACCOM. | ACCOM.
BAT. RM. | | BAT. RM.

ESCORT VESSEL (Geleitboote): *F2* — Class F1-10

Displacement	790 tons, decreased to 756 tons 1938/39
Dimensions	249.1 × 28.9 × 10.6 feet. Length increased to 263.1 feet in 1938/39
Machinery	2 sets of Brown Boveri turbines driving 2 propellers. Oil-fired. 2 experimental H.P. boilers 14,000 SHP = 28.0 kts. (design) 26.0 kts. after lengthening
Armament	2 - 4.1″,* 4 - 37mm A.A., 4 - 20mm A.A. guns. * Removed 1939 during conversion to torpedo recovery vessel.
Complement	121 officers and men
Builders	Germaniawerft, Kiel. Completed 1936

Condition of Wreck

Lying on port side, and from bow to abaft bridge in very good condition. Anchor chain running from anchor storage box over port bow cleat out to sea-bed. Forward gun turret in very good condition. On forward deck is a winch with a roll of steel cable. Stern of ship and stern part of superstructure has been blown open. Shaft and bearings can be seen, but propeller missing. Wooden barge *(YC21)* lies close alongside on sea-bed. Site of *F2* marked by red buoy.

MISCELLANEOUS WRECKAGE

Bayern's turrets — These four (main armament) turrets were torn out of the *Bayern* when she made an uncontrolled ascent in 1933. They weigh some 600 tons each and lie about 1 mile south of the Holm of Houton. Water depth 35m. Turrets lie upside down. Silty bottom. Marked as obstruction on chart.

Seydlitz — Parts of superstructure and contents of coal bunkers left at wreck site after raising of hull. Position approximately half way between Cava and Rysa Little.

Bremse — Anchor cable run ashore at Toy Ness. Miscellaneous wreckage on sea bed just off-shore.

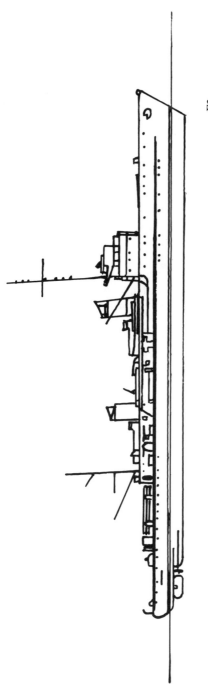

F2

The British Royal Naval wrecks date from both WWI and WWII. The largest are those of the battleships *HMS Vanguard*, sunk by accident on 9th July, 1917, and *HMS Royal Oak*, torpedoed on 13th/14th October, 1939. A minesweeper, *HMS Roedean*, sank on 13th January, 1915. Also in WWI, two tugs went down, one at Scapa and the other in Hoxa Sound.

As has previously been described, *HMS Vanguard* blew up and sank off Flotta with immense loss of life, following a magazine explosion. Although not so designated at the time, the Ministry of Defence has recently expressed the wish that the wreck site should be regarded as a war grave. In 1975, R.N. divers cleared the area as far as possible of ammunition, but given the nature of the incident and the considerable area involved, very considerable numbers of shells, etc., still remain. Divers must on no account meddle with any unidentified or suspicious objects in this area, even when operating outwith the war grave confines.

The wreck of the *HMS Royal Oak* is a formally designated war grave, and diving on her is forbidden without specific written permission from the Ministry of Defence. Two of her four 15-inch guns were subsequently salvaged and used for arming the monitors *HMS Abercrombie* and *HMS Roberts*.

HMS Roedean, a fleet minesweeper, dragged her anchor on the night of 13th January, 1915, fouled the ram of *HMS Imperieuse* (Depotship — converted armoured cruiser launched 1883), and sank (Admiralty File ADM 137/1074). The Hydrographic Department print-out of wrecks in Scapa Flow gives the cause of sinking as a mine. Readers are invited to take their pick. Originally a Great Western Railway steamer on the Weymouth - Channel Islands run, the *Roebuck* was taken into R.N. service in 1914, converted to a minesweeper and renamed *HMS Roedean*. In 1953 and 1956 clearance operations were carried out to blast off the superstructure and increase the water depth over the wreck.

The drifter *Imbat* was lost on 4th February, 1941, when she collided with another vessel (unknown) off Lyness. Built by Jones of Buckie in 1918, she was requisitioned for harbour service on 3rd October, 1939. The condition of the wreck is not known.

In addition, a further six small British Naval vessels sank in Scapa Flow during WWII. At present the position and condition of these wrecks is unknown.

Details of the British naval wrecks are listed below.

BATTLESHIP: *HMS ROYAL OAK* — ROYAL SOVEREIGN class

Displacement	Originally 25,750 tons, increased to 28,000 tons and later to 29,150 tons
Dimensions	620.4 × 88.5 × 32.5 feet. Breadth increased to 101.4 feet with the addition of anti-torpedo bulges.
Machinery	4 sets Parsons turbines driving 4 propellers Oil-fired 40,000 SHP = 23.0 kts. (design) 40,360 SHP (trial)
Armour	Main belt 10″, lower armour deck 1.75″, turrets 11″, control tower 10″ (fore), 8″ (aft)
Armament	8 - 15″ (4 × 2), 8 - 6″, 8 - 4″ A.A. guns (4 × 2), 16 - 40mm pom-poms (2 × 8), 8 - 0.5″ machine gun (2 × 4), 4 - 21″ above water T.T. (4 beam)
Complement	997 officers and men
Builders	HM Dockyard, Devonport. Completed May 1916.

Note:— *HMS Royal Oak* was extensively refitted during her life, with substantial modifications being made to her armour and armament. During the last of these refits, in 1934/35, 900 tons of armour was added to the main decks over the engine-rooms and magazines. Anti-aircraft protection was greatly strengthened, with the addition of twin-mounted high angle/low angle 4-inch guns, 40mm 8-barrel pom-poms and quadruple-barrelled 0.5-inch machine-guns.

In addition, a catapult launcher for aircraft was fitted on top of X Turret. All four submerged torpedo-tubes were removed and four new tubes fitted above water, two on each side of the ship. Radio and direction-finding equipment and fire control directors were also substantially up-dated. The *HMS Royal Oak* which sank in 1939 was a very different ship from that which was commissioned in 1916.

HMS Royal ◆
HMS Vangu

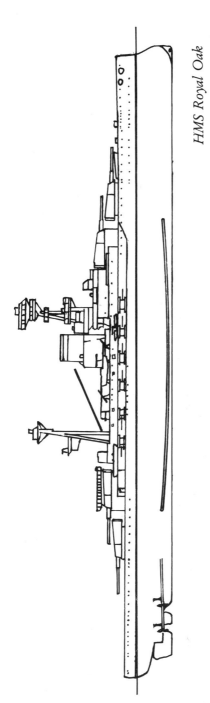

HMS Royal Oak

MD Imbat
verlane in Burra Sound

BATTLESHIP: *HMS VANGUARD* — ST VINCENT class

Displacement	19,560 tons
Dimensions	535.8 × 84.0 × 28.5 feet
Machinery	4 sets Parsons turbines driving 4 propellers
	Oil-fired
	24,500 SHP = 21 kts. (design)
	25,800 SHP = 22.1 kts. (trial)
Armour	Main belt 10″, lower armour deck 3″,
	turrets 11″, control tower 10″ (fore), 8″ (aft)
Armament	10 - 12″ (5 × 2), 12 - 4″, 4 - 3 pdr guns, 3 - 18″ submerged T.T. (2 beam, 1 stern). Total of 12-inch guns increased to 20 in 1914/15, and one stern T.T. removed in 1916.
Complement	758 officers and men
Builders	Vickers, Barrow. Completed February, 1910

Condition of Wreck

Bow pointing upwards but more or less upright. Midships blown apart. Water depth 34m. Very silty, bottom deep mud.

HMS Vanguard

FLEET MINESWEEPER: *HMS ROEDEAN* — ex *ROEBUCK*

Displacement	1094 tons gross
Dimensions	280.0 × 34.5 × 16.8 feet
Machinery	2 triple-expansion engines driving 2 propellers. Coal-fired. 19½ kts.
Armament	2 - 12 pdr.
Builders	Naval Construction and Armament Co., Barrow. Completed 1897.

Condition of Wreck

Blasted open. Boilers exposed. Water depth 15m. Bottom: silt, rock and kelp. Thick covering silt on wreck.

HM TUG: *ALEXANDRA II*

Displacement	168 tons gross
Dimensions	92.0 × 21.1 × 12.0 feet
Machinery	Compound steam twin-cylinder, single-screw
Builders	J. Cran & Co., Leith, 1907, for Alexandra Towing Co., Liverpool

HM TRAWLER: *STRATHGARY*

Tonnage	202 tons gross
Dimensions	113.0 × 21.9 × 11.7 feet
Machinery	triple-expansion engine, single-screw
Builders	Hall Russell, Aberdeen, 1906, for Aberdeen Steam Trawling and Fishing Co. Ltd.

HM TUG: *OCEANA*

Tonnage	337 tons gross
Dimensions	140.0 × 22.7 × 13.1 feet
Machinery	Compound twin-cylinder, twin-screw
Builders	Gourlay Bros., Dundee, 1889, for J. S. Watkins, London

3. MISCELLANEOUS WRECKS:

(See Table 6 and Map 3)

This is an extremely varied group, which numbers at least 14 vessels. Of these, the identities of only four are known with any certainty. The main group of nine lies scattered north of Flotta in a rectangle which extends to the Barrel of Butter. Only two of these wrecks off Flotta can be identified: the *Prudentia*, lying ½ ml due west of the Occidental Oil Terminal, and a concrete barge sunk off the north side of Flotta.

The *Prudentia* was originally a small cargo vessel of some 1,000 tons, which was chartered by the Admiralty at the beginning of WWI. She was converted into an oiler by having three tanks installed in her hold spaces. On 12th January, 1916, she dragged her mooring in bad weather, fouled *HMS Iron Duke's* buoy, and sank in 23 metres of water — ½ ml north of Gibraltar Pier, Flotta. The official report on her sinking states that she was lying on her port side on a bottom of mud and sand, and it was considered that her forward tanks were intact. Since sinking, her hull had slowly rusted, and is now severely corroded and in a very precarious state. Small amounts of oil continue to escape from her tanks and act as a marker for her position. Her transfer hoses are still on deck, but should not be touched, as they still contain considerable quantities of oil which might well be released if tampered with. She has a cast-iron propeller.

The concrete barge may be of French origin, as a considerable number of these vessels were constructed in that country to overcome a WWI steel shortage. The blockship *Naja*, sunk in 1939, was originally registered in Rouen, and might well have a sister ship. No information is available as to the condition of the wreck.

There are two miscellaneous wrecks in Gutter Sound. One, the *YC21*, lies on the sea bed close alongside the *F2*, while the other, identity unknown, is just off the Point of Cletts. A wooden barge of some 550 tons, the *YC21* sank in November 1968 during a gale, while being used on salvage work on the *F2*. The condition of the hull is unknown.

The wreck of the *James Barrie*, a trawler which sank in 1969, lies in Hoxa Sound adjacent to the entrance to Widewall Bay. She ran aground on the Louther Rock, Pentland Skerries, on 27th March, 1969, and with worsening weather the crew were taken off the 666-ton vessel shortly after. On 29th March she was found to have floated off, and was drifting derelict in the Pentland Firth. The Kirkwall Lifeboat *Grace Paterson Ritchie* took her in tow, and made for Scapa Pier, but the trawler sank suddenly off Widewall Bay. The wreck lies in 38 metres of water, and its condition is unknown.

TABLE 6
Miscellaneous Wrecks

Name	Water Depth (m)	Position
Concrete Barge	16	¾ ml E of No. 1 Jetty, Flotta.
Prudentia	23	½ ml W of No. 1 Jetty, Flotta.
James Barrie	38	1 ml S of Hoxa Head.
YC21	14	Gutter Sound F2 Buoy.
Unknown	10	Gutter Sound off Point of Cletts.
Unknown	30	1 ml N of Flotta Terminal.
4 Unknown	28-40	½-2 ml E of Cava.
Unknown	28	½ ml W of S.P.M. No. 2.
Unknown	30	1 ml SW of S.P.M. No. 1.
Unknown	36	¼ ml NW of Calf of Flotta.
Unknown	38	½ ml S of Hoxa Head.

A DIVE IN SCAPA FLOW
by Bob Michelson

Among the hustle and bustle in Stromness harbour during the summer months, one occasionally sees a group of people getting ready for a day's diving out in Scapa Flow. Aside from the diving equipment that they are stowing on-board their boat they're just like all the other people who come to the Orkney islands for their holidays. The only exception is that they are not attracted to Scapa Flow by what is to be seen above it, but rather by what is below its chilling waters: the wrecks of the German Imperial High Seas Fleet.

The one-hour run to the dive sites around the island of Cava is always filled with activity. As the dive boat gets under way each diver is busy arranging his gear for the forthcoming dive and making last-minute checks for the proper function of all of his equipment. Breathing regulators are mounted on the compressed-air bottles, pressure gauges are checked, underwater lamps and camera housings get a last going over. Are the batteries charged? Is the housing water-tight? It's better to find out now rather than when the diver is underwater. During all this activity someone had found time to fire-up the stove and the first cups of steaming hot tea are passed around.

When everyone is finished checking and arranging his equipment, the dive-master conducts his pre-dive briefing. The divers are told which ship they will be diving on, how it lies on the sea bottom, and how they can identify it. Depths and currents are mentioned, along with the necessary safety regulations which govern every diver's behaviour in the water.

The ever-present cameras are clicking, to bring

home memories of the Orkney islands with beautiful scenic shots of Graemsay and Hoy as we pass by on our way to the dive site.

With the Captain's call, "Twenty minutes to dive site," the divers start getting suited up. This is the moment of the greatest activity, and to a non-diver it looks like total confusion on board. However, the activity is very orderly as each diver and his partner help each other into their suits and gear. When everybody is suited up and ready, the dive-master makes his final check that everyone's equipment is in order. Once again the underwater cameras and housings get a final check, and by the time the Captain is ready to set his marker-buoy on the wreck, the excitement and enthusiasm for the dive is at its peak.

Due to the lack of currents and the difficulty of anchoring on the wrecks, only a marker-buoy on a shot-line is set to mark the position of the wreck. This allows the dive boat to stay mobile, and the divers are picked up in the open water where they surface; they are therefore free to explore the wrecks in their entire length and don't have to make their way back to an anchor-line.

With visibility underwater averaging 10-12 metres, we are almost on the wreck before it comes into view in its shadowy outlines, and the sheer size of the sunken vessel is overwhelming. Some of the wrecks lie on their port or starboard sides and we can orientate ourselves quickly, but on the big battleships, which are lying partly turned over and resting on their super-structures, orientation is difficult. At first we are very surprised to find the wrecks in such good condition. since only the flood-valves were opened to cause the sinking, the ships suffered little damage. The wrecks are covered with the typical growth of the northern European waters, mainly Anemone, 'Dead Man's Hands' (Soft Leather Coral), and some Kelp. Portholes and hatchways cast their magical and mystical spell, literally crying out "Come in and explore me!", but even in the shine of our powerful 100-watt lamps the interior of the ships remain black emptiness. Without the proper wreck-diving gear a penetration into these wrecks is suicidal, and we therefore limit ourselves to exploring and photographing the wrecks from the outside. We continue our way along this seemingly never-ending wreck, accompanied by the 'watchmen' of the deep, lone Codfish of majestic size or an occasional school of Mackerel or Pollock. Here we find the superstructure of the cruiser with its battle-control-tower standing away from the wreck in the emptiness of the sea. The 6-inch cannons still in their mounts point uselessly out into the water. Finning along the deck, we find the chute that leads into the coal bunkers. The deck hatch is missing and in the beam of our lights we see football-sized chunks of coal still shining on the edges as if the ship had just sunk a day ago, rather than 65 years before.

Our dive time rushes by all too quickly, and after one last check of our pressure gauges we begin our ascent. On the way to the surface and during our safety decompression stop, I start to realize how little of the giant ship I actually have seen and hope that after a few days of diving on the wrecks I will be able to orientate myself better and thus find my way around the wrecks with more ease.

One thing you can forget in your kit-bag when you come to the Orkney islands is your hammer, crowbar, chisel and wrench. Everything that wasn't screwed down has already been picked off the wrecks by previous groups of divers, and the dive operators are not allowing any divers on the wrecks with tools. Many of the local residents who worked on the big salvage jobs between 1924 and 1939 have rather large private collections of souvenirs taken from the ships, with everything from officers' sabres to soup bowls and cups. Many items can be seen in the museum in Stromness and in the private collection at Graemeshall in Holm (by the village of St Mary's), which is also open to visitors.

After our dive gear is stowed and while the tanks

are being filled for the afternoon dive we get under way
for our mid-day break at one of the many little towns
scattered around Scapa Flow. It could be to St Mary's
or Longhope or Stromness for a visit to the musuem, a
snack and a brew in one of the pubs, or we could head
for Lyness. Here was the base of operations for the
salvage firm Cox and Danks and also for Metal
Industries Ltd., who carried on after Cox and Danks
gave up operations. Lyness was also home for the
British Navy until the 1950s and a snorkel-swim or a
shallow-water dive along the pier has turned up many
an old bottle, dish or cup which was thrown off the pier
years ago. From the pier it is only a short walk to the
Royal Navy Cemetery where a number of sailors from
the German Fleet, as well as British ships, are buried.

Longhope is also an interesting stopping-place with
its two Martello Towers — stone guard-towers built
during the War of 1812 to prevent American warships
from attacking Scapa Flow. A short walk from the
towers is the Longhope Lifeboat Station where you can
see the modern rescue equipment of the Lifeboat
Service. There are pubs and shops in all the villages, and
a relaxing midday lunch and stroll is a welcome break
between dives.

We all meet back at the pier around 2 o'clock and
get under way for our second dive in the afternoon, and
generally we're back home between 5 and 6 o'clock in
the evening. For those of us who can't get enough
diving in the day's schedule, we can take a tank from
the dive boat and make a night dive along the Churchill
Barriers looking for lobsters and scallops, an interesting
way to put fresh seafood on the supper table.

I can't think of a better way to round out a day's
diving in Scapa Flow than with a meal of freshly-caught
fish or scallops and a cool beer toasting the crews of the
German Imperial High Seas Fleet and thanking them
for scuttling the ships and bringing me to the Orkney
islands to enjoy the hospitality and the diving.

25th October 1984   Hamburg

THE SCUTTLING OF THE GERMAN FLEET

Some Orcadian Eye-witness Accounts

(On the day of the sinking of the German High Seas Fleet in Scapa Flow, a party of over 150 children from Stromness were out in the Flow on a school trip. They had gone out to see the German ships, and were present at the very time when the scuttling was carried out. Over the years, several of the eye-witnesses have recorded their memories, or on tape. Amongst them was the late Mrs Ivy Scott of The Whins, Finstown, who was then a girl of 18. She later became a teacher in North Ronaldsay, where she met her husband Roy, and afterwards taught in the Rendall school. A devoted couple, they died in the summer of 1984 within a few days of each other, but earlier in the year Ivy wrote to Bob Michelson in response to a request in The Orcadian for information on the scuttling.)

It was a good day for a sea trip — a light breeze and the sun shining when we, pupils and teachers of Stromness Academy, set sail on the *Flying Kestrel*, which ran water to our fleet from the Pump Well, in Stromness. This day she embarked us all for a trip down the Flow to see the German Navy, anchored there with only a skeleton crew on board each ship. A boy from my school group lived in Lyness, so was an excellent guide, shouting in a loud voice the name, tonnage and gun power of each ship as we came along. Our headmaster, Major Hepburn, had given us instructions on how to behave in such circumstances. We simply stared, amazed. One of our party was handing round a poke of sweets, and we were all just chatting pleasantly when he — newly back and demobbed from the trenches — shouted, "What a damned cheek!!" And as we watched, down came the Union Jack and up went the German Eagle, and all around us the great ships began to sink, some on even keel and some upended and plunged down quickly and only a wash of waves to show where they had been. Suddenly the Flow came alive with drifters and smaller ships to rescue the German sailors from the sea. Some of them even managed to swim ashore. We had an extra special view, for the *Kestrel* turned round in the midst of the sinking ships — we thought to tell the *Imperieuse*, our Navy's mothership, what was happening. But we were rudely told to clear out quick, and made for Stromness under full steam. There was, as I remember, no loss of life; except that in a speed-boat a few yards away from the *Kestrel* and rushing up the Flow, a man stood up in the bow waving his arms. A man from the stern pointed, I think, a pistol. There was a puff of smoke, and the man in the bow slumped forward into the speed-boat.

What a day to remember! And what a tale we had to tell!

(Amongst the many classic recordings made by the late Ernest W. Marwick was a interview with the late Mr and Mrs William Groundwater of Stromness. William Groundwater was the Rector of Stromness Academy, and Mrs Rosetta Groundwater was Provost of the town. Many years before, they had both been aboard the Flying Kestrel on her historic trip through the Flow.)

WG: Well, so far as the weather is concerned, first, I should say it was a lovely summer day and we all enjoyed the trip very much. We got down through the boom gates a Houton, and then we sailed right in to the midst of the German Fleet. Of course, we were all excited to see them, and watching them, and in the process it began to be gradually realised that some of the ships were sinking a bit lower in the water. At the same time we noticed a lot of activity on the ships. I remember seeing some of the sailors dragging their kit and some of them dragging rafts and throwing them over. Everyone by this time was getting very excited and wondering what was happening. It slowly dawned on us that something extraordinary was happening and that the ships were actually beginning to sink.

British destroyers began to steam round, and some British trawlers as well. I remember some of the sailors jumping down onto the rafts from the ships. You could see some of their boats and rafts floating on the water and I remember hearing at least one rifle shot.

Everything was beginning to get very exciting by that time; it was like a kind of slow-motion picture. The ships then began to sink — to sink lower in the water — to turn turtle. Some of them went down by the stern and everybody, of course, I imagine, was almost speechless with excitement at that time — all eyes watching what was happening.

RG: I think at this stage we were ordered back to the depot ship to get orders what to do, but as we went to the depot ship, I distinctly saw the *Seydlitz* turn turtle and the water come streaming out of the sea-cocks and the activity was just tremendous.

Men were in boats, and I definitely saw one man shot. He dropped right out of the stern of the boat. The other men were standing with their hands up. I presume it was surrender.

We were evidently in a difficult position, or in danger, and we were ordered out of the way.

EWM: How near were you to the ships then?

RG: Oh, we were right in among them — they were sinking at each side of us. The *Seydlitz* would have been just a few hundred yards away, when it turned turtle. We had to stop, I remember, at one stage, and then we evidently were given a direction — how to get back to the depot ship. We stayed there for a bit and the captain seemed to get some orders to go a different route back, because we went way outside where the ships were the next time.

But to us it just seemed to be an adventure story we had been reading. We didn't understand that it was a piece of history we were seeing enacted. We thought it was just put on, probably for our benefit as school-children.

(Also aboard the Flying Kestrel that day was Mrs Peggie Gibson of Kirkwall, then 10-year-old Peggie Matheson, one of four sisters on the trip. She recorded her account of the events for Ernest Marwick in the 1960s, and then in 1984 for Kathryn Gourlay of Radio Orkney.)

We had been told that the British Fleet would be there, as well as the German Fleet. We were quite a distance down, when we began to see German destroyers lying in pairs, all the way down. Then a trawler came along and with a megaphone shouted "The German Fleet are sinking — make for the *Victorious.*"

So the captain of the *Flying Kestrel* must have decided to go on, which he did. We had a most spectacular view of the fleet sinking — some sank into the water, some stood up on their bows and turned over, and some went over by their side. The water was boiling everywhere and men were about on rafts and boats. We saw them landing on the island of Cava and running up from the shore.

One thing I've always remembered was that every German boat had its flag at top mast, while they were sinking.

We went alongside the *Victorious* and there was a trawler there, collecting the captains and the officers off the German ships. We could see them all in a boat with sailors, who had guns. The captains were all taken and put into this boat and were held there. It was a most amazing sight for children to see.

Now during the time we were there you can imagine what it must have been like for the parents in Stromness — the anxiety: "The children are visiting the fleet, the boat's not in and the German Fleet are sinking." I guess that there was quite a lot of panic in

Stromness about that time, and I know that when we happily returned to Stromness that evening, every pier was crowded with people watching for the boat to come back. But we all arrived home safely and were greatly thrilled with this adventure that we had had.

KG: Were you in the middle of it — were they all around you?

PG: Yes, all around. I myself saw twelve different ships. We were counting them to see how many we could see. I saw twelve go down. The competition on the boat, among the pupils, was to see how many of the names of the ships we could get. We had started to take down the names as we went, but before we reached the main fleet, there were so many of them sinking, it was difficult.

KG: Did you see the life-boats being launched off them too?

PG: Oh yes, we saw them, and sometimes a raft. We were sorry for the men, of course, because they were getting washed with the waves and there were so few. You would see quite a few men on the raft and then you would see three left and so on, but I think a great many of them were able to get to the shore. The island — Cava — seemed to be covered with men, anyway.

KG: Were the German captains very proud?

PG: As a child I thought, why shouldn't they go down with their flags flying, even though they had been conquered. We felt sorry for them, you see — we felt sorry for those that were in the sea and the struggle with the ships. Being children, we didn't think of them as being an enemy.

(In 1984 Bob Michelson visited Orkney with a German TV team, to make a film on the sunken fleet in Scapa Flow. They were particularly interested in meeting eye-witnesses of the scuttling, and organised a boat trip in

Scapa Flow with three of the people who had been out there on the Flying Kestrel, 65 years before: the late Willie Marwick, Mrs Kitty Tait, and J. R. T. Robertson, Orkney Islands Councillor for Sandwick and a former Provost of the town of Stromness. Kitty Tait and her husband Sandy were in Orkney in the Second World War when on one occasion machine-gun bullets from a German plane raiding the Flow ricocheted off their roof, in the South End of Stromness. Willie Marwick, who was an 8-year-old boy at the time of the scuttling, went on to work on the salvage of the German Fleet with Cox and Danks, and had a lifelong interest in their ships and their story. On a summer day in 1984, Kathryn Gourlay went out in the Flow with the group, to record their conversation as the events of 21st June 1919 were recalled.)

KT: I can remember the time we left the pier — it was a beautiful day and we sailed away very triumphantly and feeling very important. Everything was going well and we were excited to be on this, what we thought was a big boat then, and suddenly there was a great motion among the fleet. We were looking at them and I saw what I would say would be one of the biggest ships — suddenly it shuddered and shuddered and shuddered, and then suddenly it toppled over and I can remember seeing Germans coming off on rafts. I seem to remember all the other ships — the water cascading up all around us.

WM: When we were going down in the *Flying Kestrel*, we were all standing on the deck. We closed round the ships and eventually we saw the one gradually getting deeper in the water, and eventually she went down by the stern. the other ones then — they started to keel over and there were some of the boats — they managed to get some of them ashore, of the destroyers. The rest of them, they just went down one after the other. It was a terrific sight to see: I felt frightened.

KT: Oh, I was terrified.

WM: There was great excitement — we all got scared because we didn't know what was going to happen, and of course eventually they told us that they were going to take us back up to Stromness. That was the last we saw of the ships.

JRTR: On the way back we passed the sinking ships, very close to, and saw what appeared to be hundreds of men on the surface swimming. As we looked further away, we heard small arms fire — machine-guns. I can still hear it, and heavier guns; and eventually, of course, we got back to Stromness.

KT: At the time that they were sinking the ships, my own mother was at the end of the pier and my eldest brother was home on leave out of the Navy. He was lying in bed, and of course they were all up the wall about us down there — frightened we were going to be pulled under with the suction of the ships going down. She surely ran upstairs to this older brother and shouted, "James Robert, do you know what the Germans are doing?"

"No."

"They're sinking their ships rather than let the British get them, or the French or any of the Allies."

And he just said, "Yes, Mother, if that had been the British you would have said — 'What brave men'."

—*Compiled by Howie Firth at BBC Radio Orkney from the Orkney Sound Archive. Tape transcriptions by Miss Fiona Scott, Burray.*

Thanks are expressed to Mr Rognvald Scott, Mr Billy Groundwater, Mrs Peggie Gibson, Mr Colin Marwick, Mrs Kitty Tait and Councillor J. R. T. Robertson for their kind permission to use these extracts and help in making them available.

BIBLIOGRAPHY

Beesley Patrick, *Room 40: British Naval Intelligence 1914-18*, Hamish Hamilton, London, 1982.

Bowman G., *The Man Who Bought a Navy*, Harrap, London, 1964.

Breyer S., *Battleships and Battlecruisers 1905-1970*, Macdonald and Jane's, London, 1973.

British Vessels Lost at Sea 1939-45, Patrick Stephens, Cambridge, 1983.

Brown M. and Meehan P., *Scapa Flow*, Allen Lane, London, 1968.

Burrows C. W., *Scapa and a Camera*, Country Life, London, 1921.

Chart 35, Scapa Flow and Northern Approaches, Hydrographic Department, Ministry of Defence, Taunton, 1980.

Colledge, J. J., *Ships of the Royal Navy*, David and Charles, Newton Abbot, 1970, 2 vols.

Conway's All the World's Fighting Ships 1922-1946, Conway Maritime Press, London, 1980.

Cousins G., *The Story of Scapa Flow*, Muller, London, 1965.

Crouther Gordon, T., *Early Flying in Orkney: Seaplanes in World War One*, BBC Radio Orkney, Kirkwall 1985.

Davidson M., Wrecks, rocks and rösts of Orkney, *Scottish Diver*, July-August, 1983.

Dittmar F. J. and Colledge J. J., *British Warships 1914 - 1919*, Ian Allan, London, 1972.

Duckworth C. L. D. and Langmuir G. E., *West Highland Steamers*, T. Stephenson and Sons Ltd., Preston, Lancashire, 1967.

Duckworth C. L. D. and Langmuir G. E., *Railway and Other Steamers*, T. Stephenson and Sons Ltd., Prescot, Lancashire, 1968.

George S. C., *Jutland to Junkyard*, Patrick Stephens, Cambridge, 1973.

Gibson R. H. and Prendergast M., *The German Submarine War, 1914 to 1918*, London, 1931.

Grant, Robert M., *U-boats Destroyed: the Effects of Anti-submarine Warfare 1914 - 1918*, Putnam, London, 1964.

Grant, Robert M., *U-boat Intelligence 1914 - 1918*, Putnam, London, 1969.

Gray, Edwyn A., *The Killing Time: the U-boat War, 1914 - 18*, London, 1972.

Gröner E., *Die deutchen Kriegsschiffe 1815-1945*, J. F. Lehmann's Verlag, Munich, 1966.

Herwig, Holger H., *Luxury Fleet, The Imperial German Navy 1888 - 1918*, Allen & Unwin, London, 1980.

Hewison, W. S., *Scapa Flow — The Navy's Northern Base*, The Orkney Press, Stromness, 1985.

Jane's Fighting Ships, 1914, 1919 and 1939.

Lloyds Register for Shipping, 1894-95, 1905-06, 1912-13, 1913-14, 1915-16, 1918-19, 1937-38, 1939-40, 1940-41, 1941-42.

Marsh, Edgar J., *British Destroyers 1892 - 1953*, Seeley Service, London, 1966.

North Coasts of Scotland Pilot, Hydrographic Department, Taunton, 1975.

North Sea Pilot, Volume 1, Hydrographic Department, London, 1960.

Orcadian and *Orkney Herald* for 1914, 1918-25, 1938 and 1939.

Parkes O., *British Battleships 1860-1950*, Seeley Service, London, 1973.

Pottinger J., *The Salving of the German Fleet*, Stromness Museum, 1975.

Preston A., *Battleships of World War I*, Arms and Armour Press, London, 1972.

Raven A., and Robert J., *British Battleships of World War II*, Arms and Armour Press, London, 1980.

Return of Shipping Casualties and Loss of Life for Period Ended 31 December 1918, Cmd. 1089, H.M.S.O., London, 1981.

Rössler E., *The U-boat*, Arms and Armour Press, London, 1981.

Ruge Vice Admiral F., *Scapa Flow 1919: the end of the German Fleet*, Ian Allan, London, 1973.

Snyder, Gerald S., *The Royal Oak Disaster*, William Kimber, London, 1976.

Sutherland Graeme, P. N., "Graeme Spence, Scapa Flow in 1812 — A memorial to the Lords commissioners of the Admiralty," *An Orkney Miscellany*, Orkney Record and Antiquarian Society, Kirkwall, 1954.

Taylor J. C., *German Warships of World War I*, Ian Allan, London, 1971.

Taylor J. C., *German Warships of World War II*, Ian Allan, London, 1966.

van der Vat D., *The Grand Scuttle*, Hodder and Stoughton, London, 1982.

Weaver, H. J., *Nightmare at Scapa Flow: the truth about the sinking of HMS Royal Oak*, Cressrelles Publishing Co., Oxfordshire, 1980.

Official sources include Cabinet and Admiralty files lodged at the Public Record Office, Kew, covering the defence of Scapa Flow in WWI and WWII; the internment, scuttling and salvage of the German High Seas Fleet, the sinking of *HMS Vanguard* and *HMS Royal Oak,* and the sinking of various smaller ships in Scapa Flow in both World Wars.

STROMNESS MUSEUM

Hundreds of divers each year make a pilgrimage through the narrow, winding street to see the German Fleet Exhibition at Stromness Museum. Here, vividly portrayed, is the story of the scuttling and salvage of one of the world's greatest war fleets.

The photograph collection has been built up from many sources. The ships are seen steaming in endless procession to their last anchorage around the low islands of Scapa Flow. Pictures taken during internment show dispirited German sailors lounging on deck or fishing to supplement their rations, while the ships moulder and rust.

By some miracle a good photographer was on hand on 21st June 1919 to record the death-throes of the ships as they reared and plunged to the sea-bed. The spectacular salvage operations of the next two decades were front page news, and photographers were commissioned to record them. One of the best was Willie Hourston of Stromness, whose work figures prominently in the exhibition.

The items on display are many and varied. The largest is a metal wash-stand reputedly from the destroyer *G89* which was broken up in Stromness Harbour by the Stromness Salvage Syndicate. On a shelf above the gleaming metal basin is a pocket mirror with the name 'Fracko', a shaving brush and a razor. The heaviest item must be the great cast-iron bell with the name *SMS Dresden* embossed on its side.

The many items of brass include a ship's telegraph and a chronometer. A collection of engine-room name-plates has been presented by a former salvage operator.

Crested china, beer mugs and cutlery evoke life below decks, and a water-stained diary records a sailor's feelings of despondency on arrival at Scapa Flow. Sailors' hatbands announce   *SMS Dresden, SMS Prinz Regent Luitpold, SMS Cöln, SMS Hindenburg, SMS Markgraf.* . . . Above all hangs the German Ensign which was struck on the foremast of *Hindenburg* when she was scuttled.

The Museum is appropriately situated on a pier to portray Orkney's Maritime History, of which the German Fleet is only one layer in a very rich cake. Displays recall the great days of the Hudson's Bay Company whose ships made Stromness their last port of call; the regular visits of the whaling vessels en route for the Davis Straits; the herring boats which thronged Orkney's harbours at the turn of the century; the wrecks which litter our coasts and the lighthouses and lifeboats which have saved many lives. There is also a superb collection of photographs of Stromness and Stromness folk in the late 19th and early 20th centuries.

The Natural History Section contains fine collections of local birds and their eggs, mammals, butterflies and moths, shells and crustacea, fossils and plants.

The Orkney Natural History Society founded the Museum in 1837. It publishes books and booklets on Orkney history, and these are on sale along with other souvenirs. Membership of the Society at a small annual fee helps support the Museum.

The Museum is open all year, apart from 3 weeks in February, and public holidays and Sundays. It is also closed on Thursday afternoons, except in July and August. Opening times: 1100-12.30, 1330-1700. (July and August open 10.30)

THE SCAPA FLOW PROJECT

The undersea features of Scapa Flow are matched in scale by those on land. During the First World War, fuel tanks and shore facilities were provided at Lyness for the Royal Navy's Grand Fleet anchored in the Flow. On the outbreak of the Second World War, the Navy returned to Scapa Flow, which became the base for the Home Fleet. After the sinking of *HMS Royal Oak* by the *U47* and the bombing of *HMS Iron Duke* in October 1939, Scapa Flow was heavily fortified and Lyness was greatly expanded to become a major naval base with fuel tanks, dockyard facilities, piers, wharfs, ammunition dumps and a major wireless communications centre.

During the war years, thousands of servicemen and women were stationed at Lyness and the numerous camps around Scapa Flow. The White Ensign of the Royal Navy was lowered for the last time at Lyness in 1957, and with the passing years the base gradually became derelict.

In April 1977 Orkney Islands Council purchased the former base from the Ministry of Defence and a Lyness Development Plan was prepared. In 1984, with joint funding from the Council and the Scottish Development Agency, a major programme of site clearance and land rehabilitation commenced at Lyness. The Council quickly recognised the importance of the Lyness Base and Sçapa Flow as part of Orkney and the Nation's heritage, and decided to retain one of the 16 oil tanks, together with the Second World War Pumphouse and important wartime artefacts. The Council, in association with the Scottish Development Agency and the Highlands and Islands Development Board, proposes to create a Scapa Flow Interpretation Centre, based on the Pumphouse and Tank at Lyness, which will tell the story of "Scapa Flow in the Defence of Britain" and direct visitors to key wartime sites in Orkney.

This imaginative project, which is being co-ordinated by the Council's Planning Department, is attracting support from a wide range of organisations and individuals and already a number of artefacts have been donated for display at Lyness.

SCAPA FLOW — THE NAVY'S NORTHERN BASE

The complete story of the famous Orkney anchorage is told, from the days before the Norsemen, through to the present day when tankers load North Sea oil. The Flow was a vital strategic base for Britain's Navy in two World Wars and became the temporary home for many thousands of service men and women.

From Scapa Flow the Grand Fleet sailed in 1916 to do battle with the German High Seas Fleet at Jutland. It was from the Flow that the cruiser *Hampshire* set off on her ill-fated final mission, with Lord Kitchener on board. Three years later, the German High Seas Fleet, interned in Scapa Flow, was scuttled by its officers and crew.

Weaknesses in the Flow's defences were exposed in the early days of World War Two, when the German submarine *U47* entered the Flow to torpedo the *Royal Oak*. The Churchill Barriers were built to seal the eastern side of Scapa Flow, and massive anti-aircraft barrages were developed. The Flow is part of Britain's naval history, and its story is told here by the former Chief Reporter of *The Orcadian,* who himself served on the Scapa defences in World War Two.

ISBN 0 907618 11 1   £12